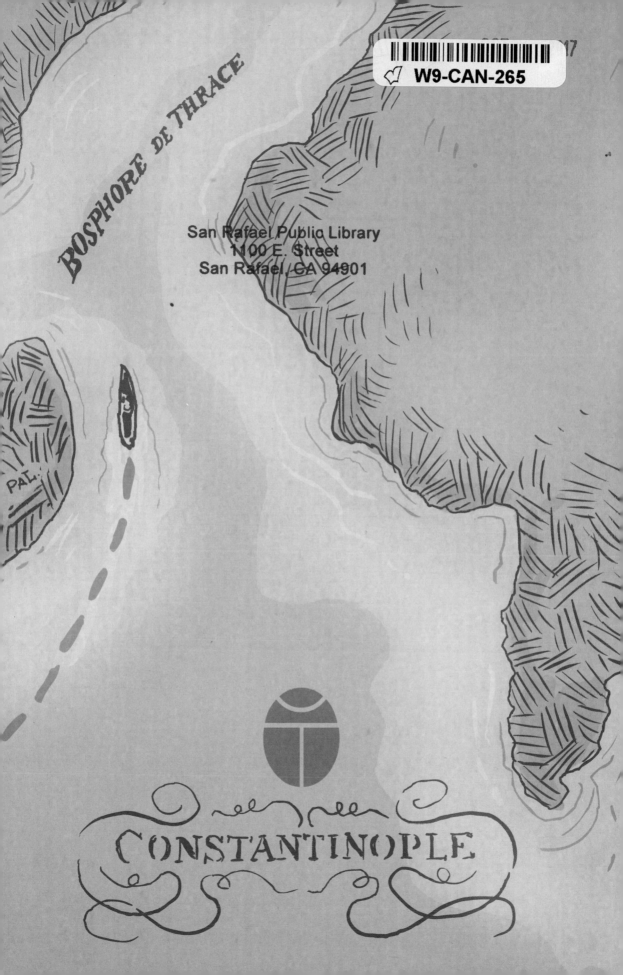

San Rafael Public Library
1100 E. Street
San Rafael, CA 94901

W9-CAN-265

THE BLACK BEETLE

™

T.M ® © 2013 FRANCESCO FRANCAVILLA

THE BLACK BEETLE

IN

Kara

Letters by
NATE PIEKOS of **BLAMBOT**®

Cover by
FRANCESCO FRANCAVILLA

The Black Beetle created by
FRANCESCO FRANCAVILLA

Dark Horse Books

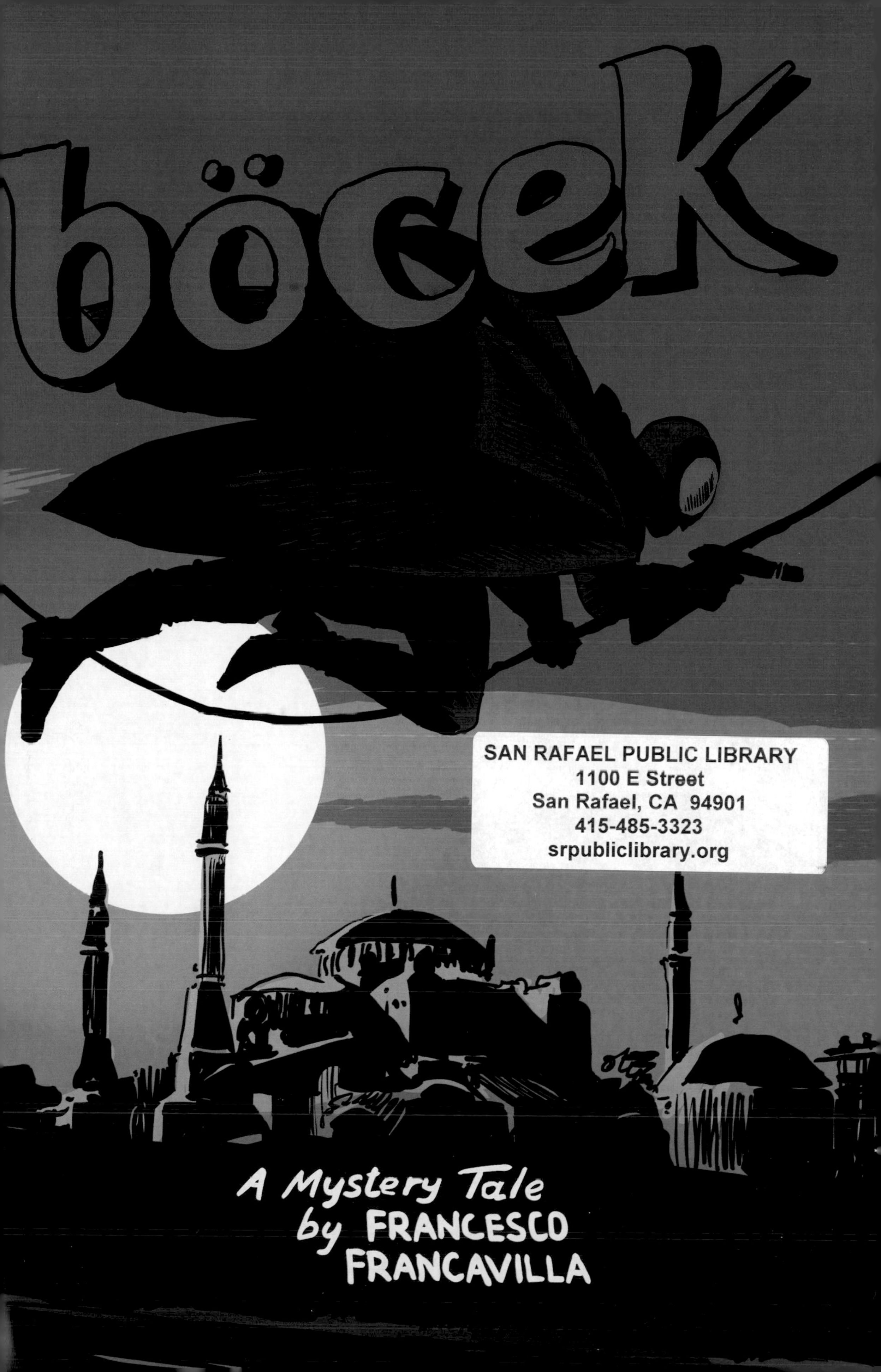
böcek
A Mystery Tale
by FRANCESCO
FRANCAVILLA

Publisher
MIKE RICHARDSON

Editor
SCOTT ALLIE

Assistant Editor
KATII O'BRIEN

Cover Designer
FRANCESCO FRANCAVILLA

Collection Designers
FRANCESCO FRANCAVILLA and **PATRICK SATTERFIELD**

Digital Art Technician
ALLYSON HALLER

Special Thanks to Lisa Francavilla for editorial assistance and continuous support.
Thanks to Scott Allie, Katii O'Brien, Mike Richardson, Jim Gibbons, and Elisabeth Allie.

Published by
Dark Horse Books
A division of Dark Horse Comics, Inc.
10956 SE Main Street • Milwaukie, OR 97222

DarkHorse.com

International Licensing (503) 905-2377 • Comic Shop Locator Service (888) 266-4226

This volume collects *The Black Beetle: Kara Böcek* parts 1–5 from *Dark Horse Presents* (volume 3) #28–#32.

10 9 8 7 6 5 4 3 2 1
Printed in China

First edition: September 2017
ISBN 978-1-50670-537-8

Neil Hankerson Executive Vice President • Tom Weddle Chief Financial Officer • Randy Stradley Vice President of Publishing • Matt Parkinson Vice President of Marketing • David Scroggy Vice President of Product Development • Dale LaFountain Vice President of Information Technology • Cara Niece Vice President of Production and Scheduling • Nick McWhorter Vice President of Media Licensing • Mark Bernardi Vice President of Book Trade and Digital Sales • Ken Lizzi General Counsel • Dave Marshall Editor in Chief • Davey Estrada Editorial Director • Scott Allie Executive Senior Editor • Chris Warner Senior Books Editor • Cary Grazzini Director of Specialty Projects • Lia Ribacchi Art Director • Vanessa Todd Director of Print Purchasing • Matt Dryer Director of Digital Art and Prepress • Sarah Robertson Director of Product Sales • Michael Gombos Director of International Publishing and Licensing

THE BLACK BEETLE: KARA BÖCEK

The Black Beetle™ © 2016, 2017 Francesco Francavilla. Dark Horse Books® and the Dark Horse logo are registered trademarks of Dark Horse Comics, Inc. All rights reserved. No portion of this publication may be reproduced or transmitted, in any form or by any means, without the express written permission of Dark Horse Comics, Inc. Names, characters, places, and incidents featured in this publication either are the product of the author's imagination or are used fictitiously. Any resemblance to actual persons (living or dead), events, institutions, or locales, without satiric intent, is coincidental.

Library of Congress Cataloging-in-Publication Data

Names: Francavilla, Francesco, author, artist. | Piekos, Nate, letterer.
Title: Black Beetle : Kara Bocek, a mystery tale / by Francesco Francavilla ; letters by Nate Piekos of Blambot ; cover by Francesco Francavilla.
Description: First edition. | Milwaukie, OR : Dark Horse Books, 2017. | "The Black Beetle created by Francesco Francavilla." | "This volume collects The Black Beetle: Kara Bocek parts 1-5 from Dark Horse Presents Volume 3 #28-#32."
Identifiers: LCCN 2017015518 | ISBN 9781506705378
Subjects: LCSH: Comic books, strips, etc.
Classification: LCC PN6728.B518 F73 2017 | DDC 741.5/973–dc23
LC record available at https://lccn.loc.gov/2017015518

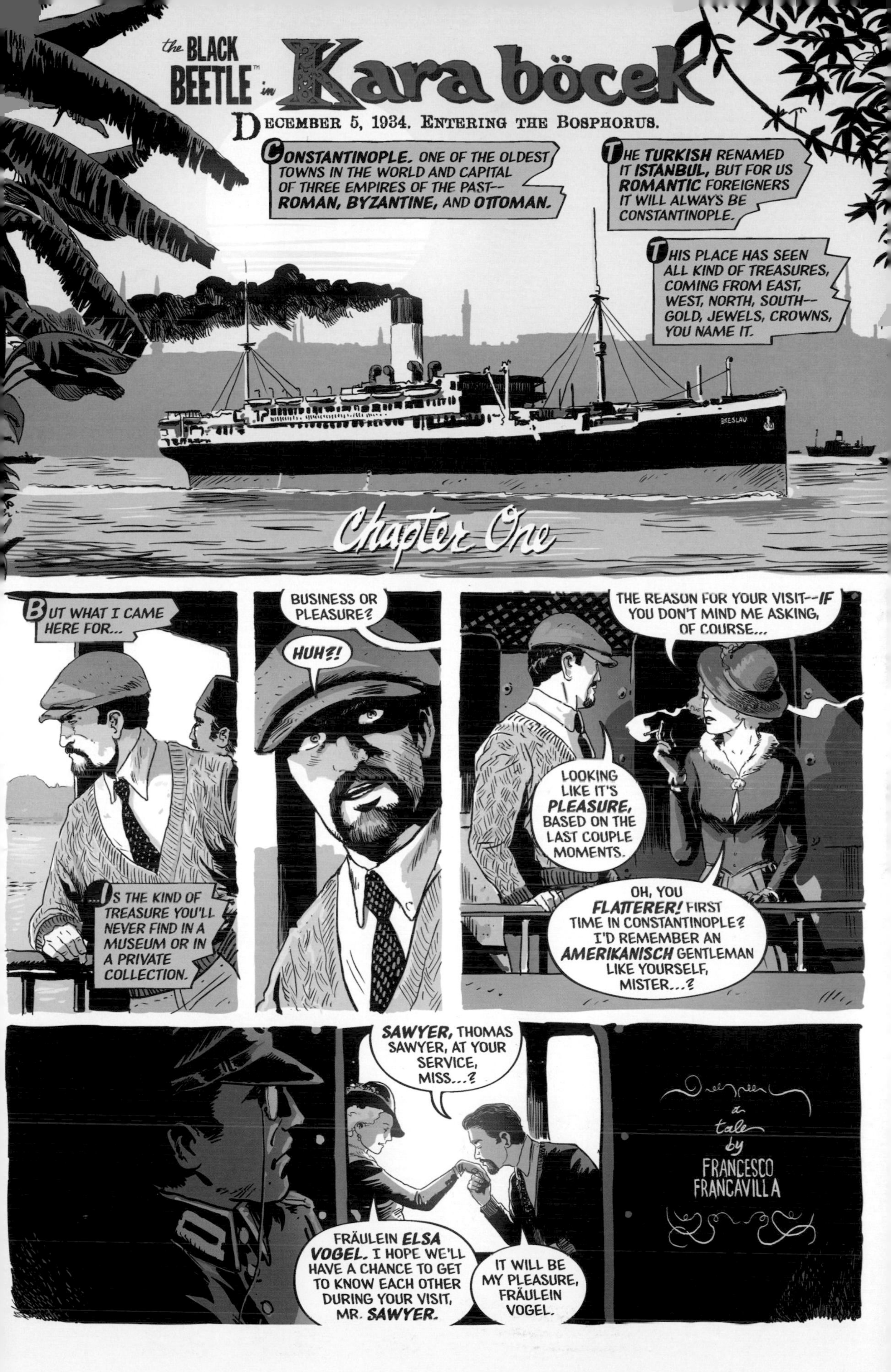

the BLACK BEETLE™ in Kara böcek
DECEMBER 5, 1934. ENTERING THE BOSPHORUS.
CONSTANTINOPLE. ONE OF THE OLDEST TOWNS IN THE WORLD AND CAPITAL OF THREE EMPIRES OF THE PAST-- ROMAN, BYZANTINE, AND OTTOMAN.
THE TURKISH RENAMED IT ISTANBUL, BUT FOR US ROMANTIC FOREIGNERS IT WILL ALWAYS BE CONSTANTINOPLE.
THIS PLACE HAS SEEN ALL KIND OF TREASURES, COMING FROM EAST, WEST, NORTH, SOUTH-- GOLD, JEWELS, CROWNS, YOU NAME IT.
BRESLAU
Chapter One
BUT WHAT I CAME HERE FOR...
IS THE KIND OF TREASURE YOU'LL NEVER FIND IN A MUSEUM OR IN A PRIVATE COLLECTION.
BUSINESS OR PLEASURE?
HUH?!
THE REASON FOR YOUR VISIT--IF YOU DON'T MIND ME ASKING, OF COURSE...
LOOKING LIKE IT'S PLEASURE, BASED ON THE LAST COUPLE MOMENTS.
OH, YOU FLATTERER! FIRST TIME IN CONSTANTINOPLE? I'D REMEMBER AN AMERIKANISCH GENTLEMAN LIKE YOURSELF, MISTER...?
SAWYER, THOMAS SAWYER, AT YOUR SERVICE, MISS...?
FRÄULEIN ELSA VOGEL. I HOPE WE'LL HAVE A CHANCE TO GET TO KNOW EACH OTHER DURING YOUR VISIT, MR. SAWYER.
IT WILL BE MY PLEASURE, FRÄULEIN VOGEL.
a tale by FRANCESCO FRANCAVILLA

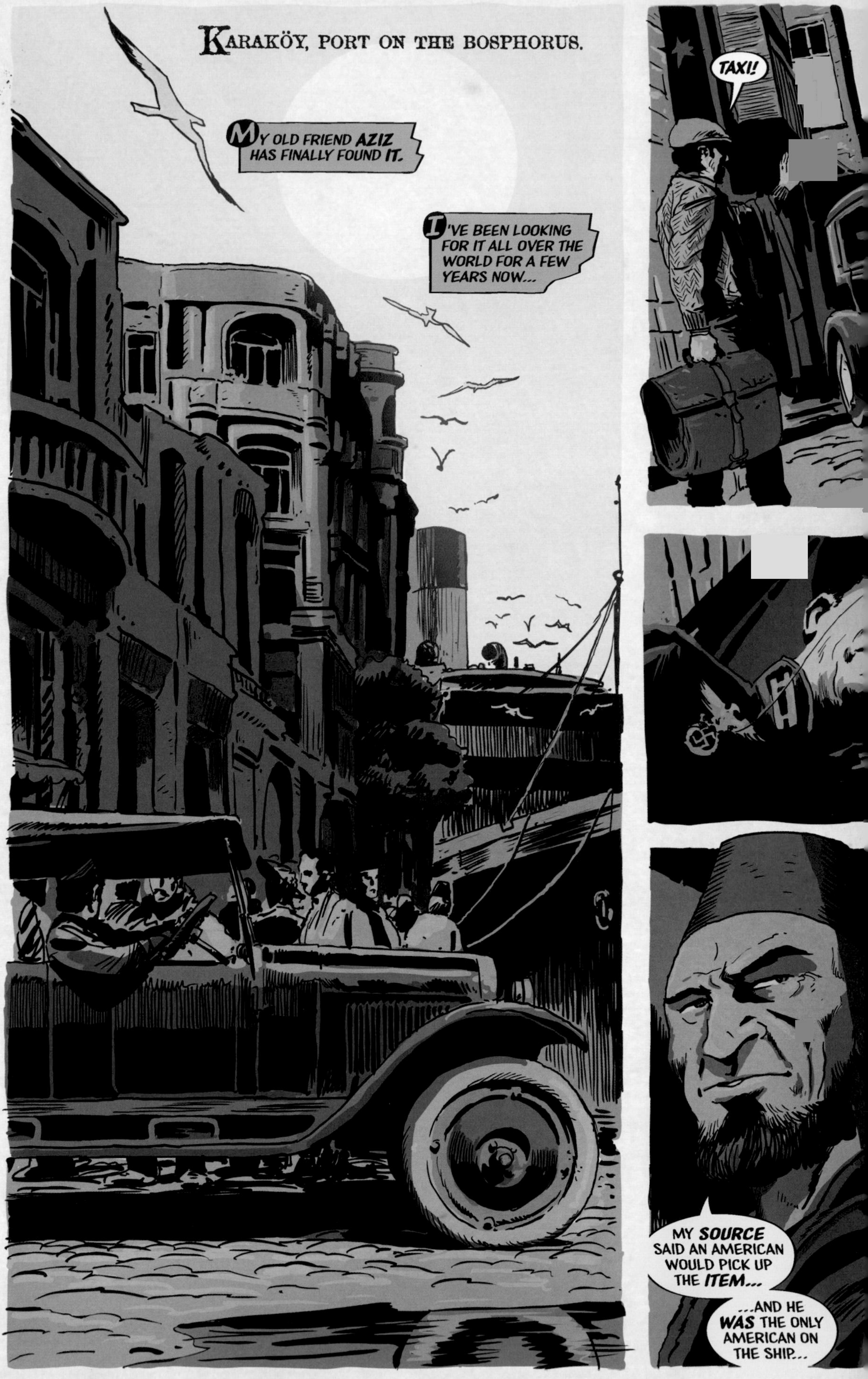
KARAKÖY, PORT ON THE BOSPHORUS.
MY OLD FRIEND AZIZ HAS FINALLY FOUND IT.
I'VE BEEN LOOKING FOR IT ALL OVER THE WORLD FOR A FEW YEARS NOW...
TAXI!
MY SOURCE SAID AN AMERICAN WOULD PICK UP THE ITEM...
...AND HE WAS THE ONLY AMERICAN ON THE SHIP...

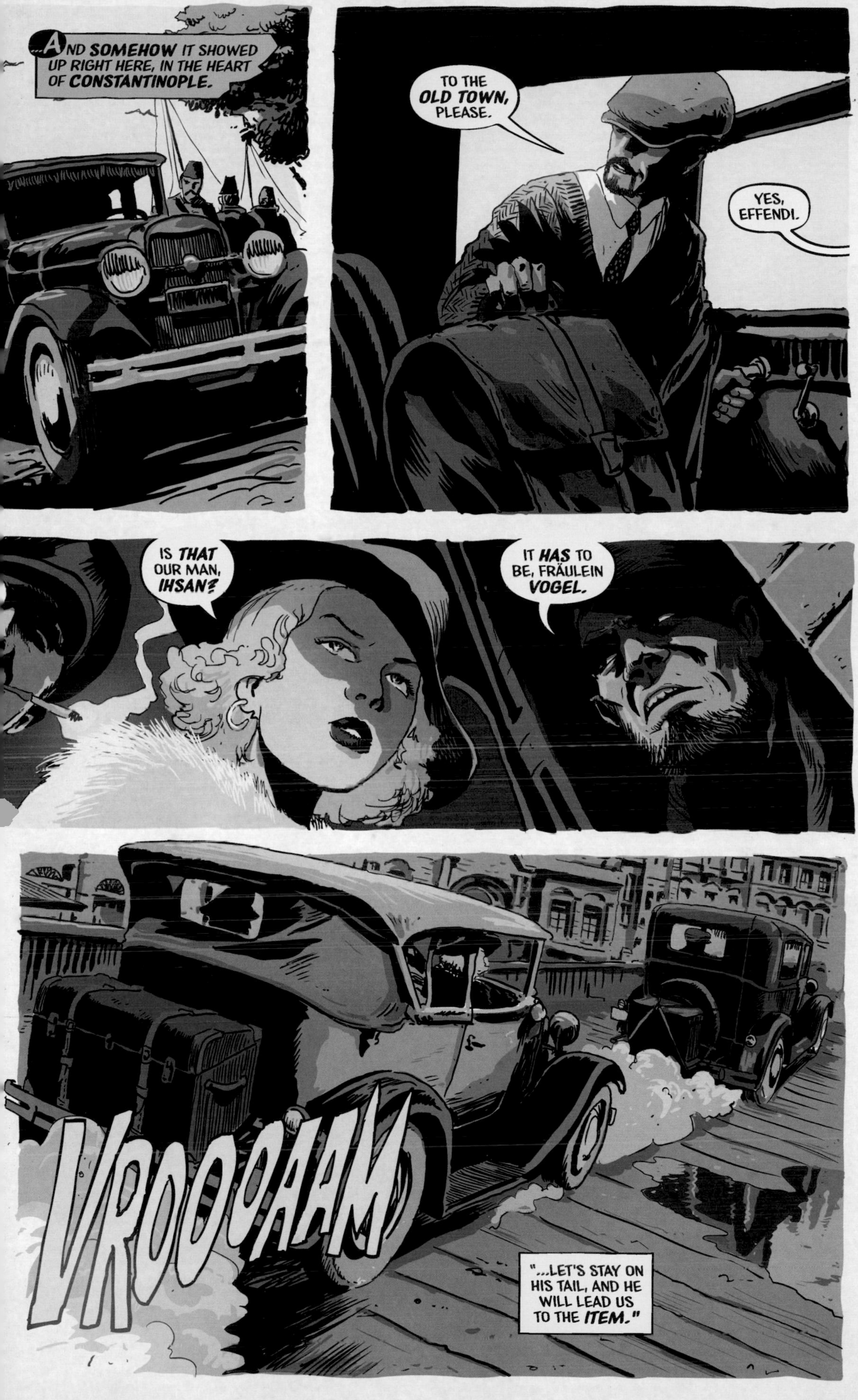
...AND SOMEHOW IT SHOWED UP RIGHT HERE, IN THE HEART OF CONSTANTINOPLE.
TO THE OLD TOWN, PLEASE.
YES, EFFENDI.
IS THAT OUR MAN, IHSAN?
IT HAS TO BE, FRÄULEIN VOGEL.
VROOOAAM
"...LET'S STAY ON HIS TAIL, AND HE WILL LEAD US TO THE ITEM."

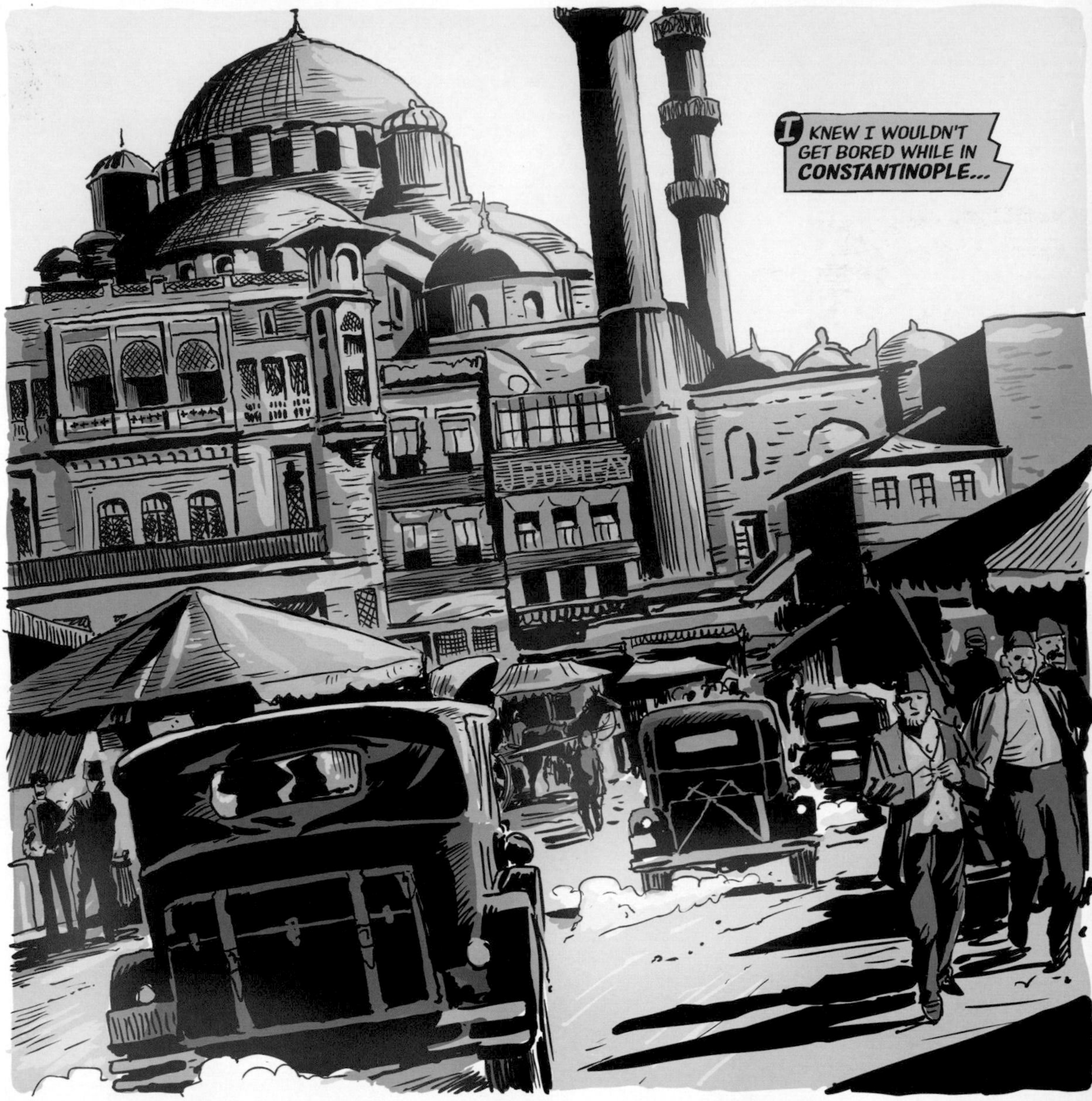
I KNEW I WOULDN'T GET BORED WHILE IN CONSTANTINOPLE...

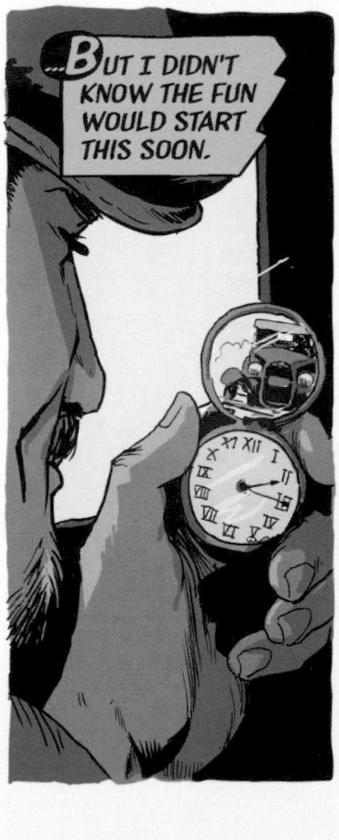
...BUT I DIDN'T KNOW THE FUN WOULD START THIS SOON.

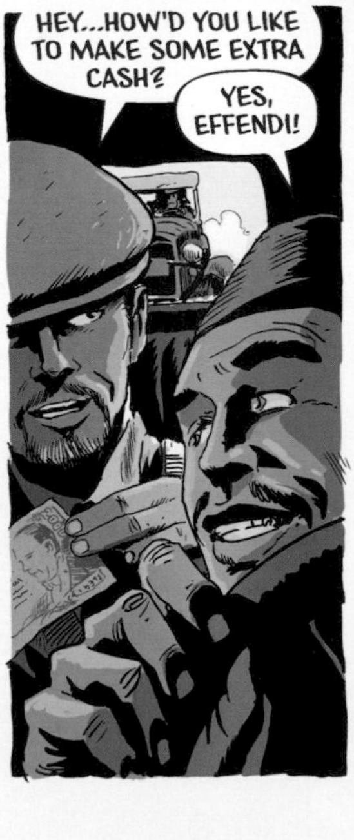
HEY...HOW'D YOU LIKE TO MAKE SOME EXTRA CASH?
YES, EFFENDI!

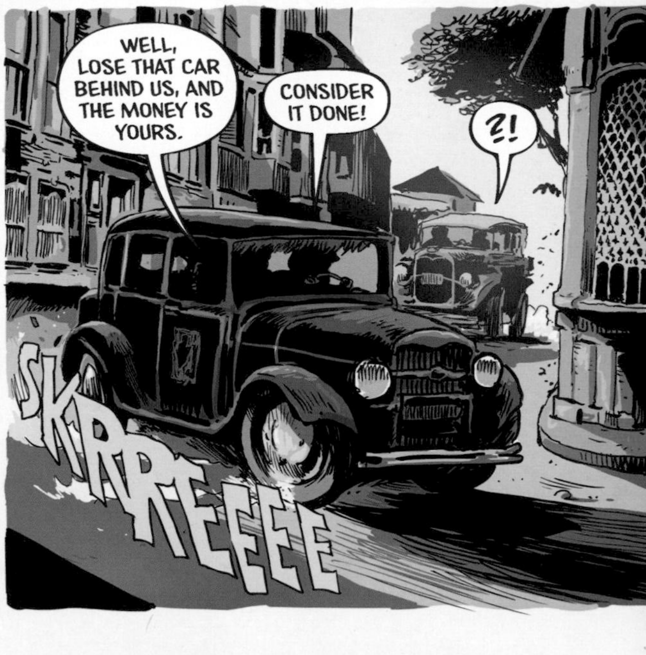
WELL, LOSE THAT CAR BEHIND US, AND THE MONEY IS YOURS.
CONSIDER IT DONE!
?!
SKRREEEEE

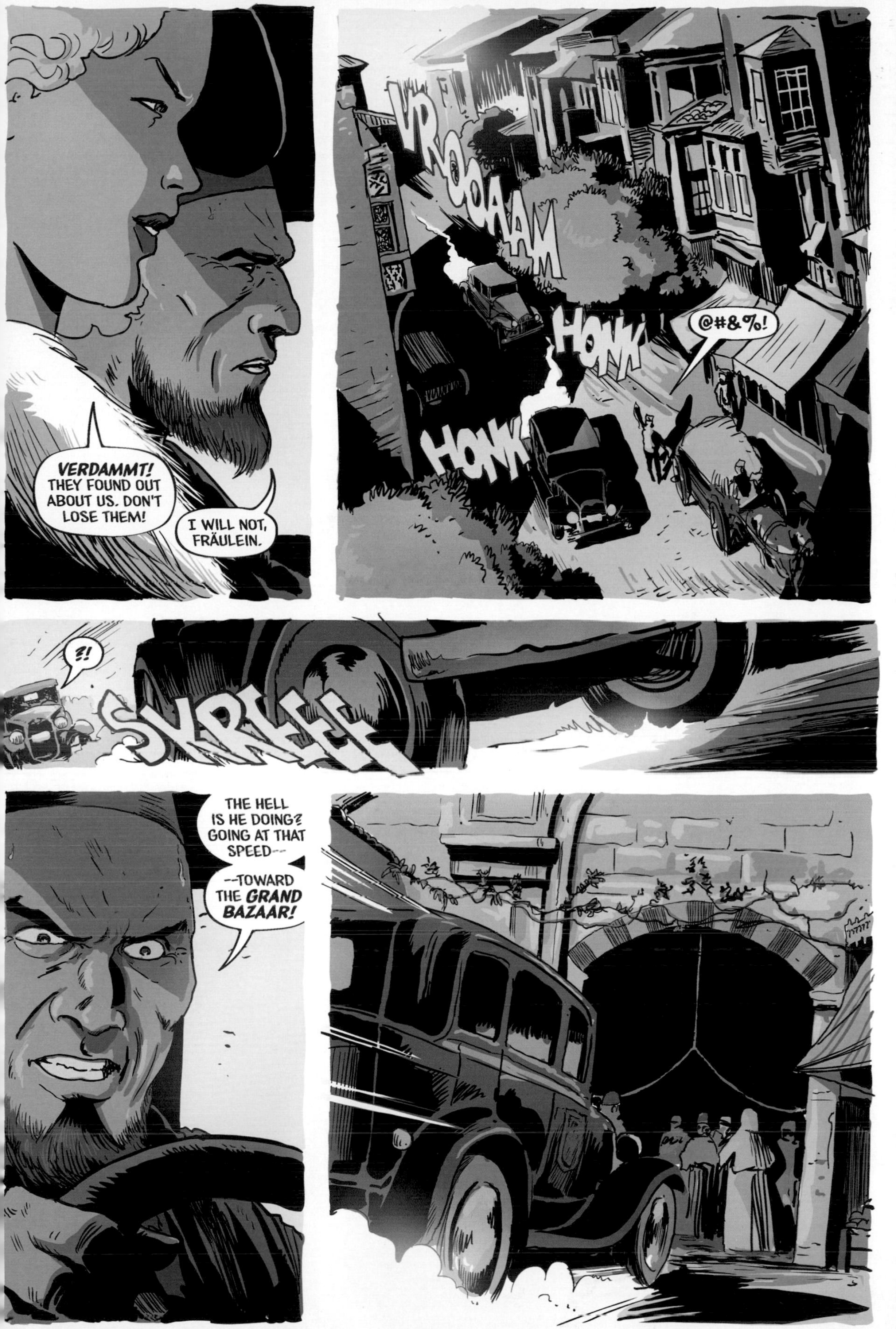
VERDAMMT! THEY FOUND OUT ABOUT US. DON'T LOSE THEM!
I WILL NOT, FRÄULEIN.
VROOAAAM
HONK
@#&%!
HONK
?!
SKREEE
THE HELL IS HE DOING? GOING AT THAT SPEED--
--TOWARD THE GRAND BAZAAR!

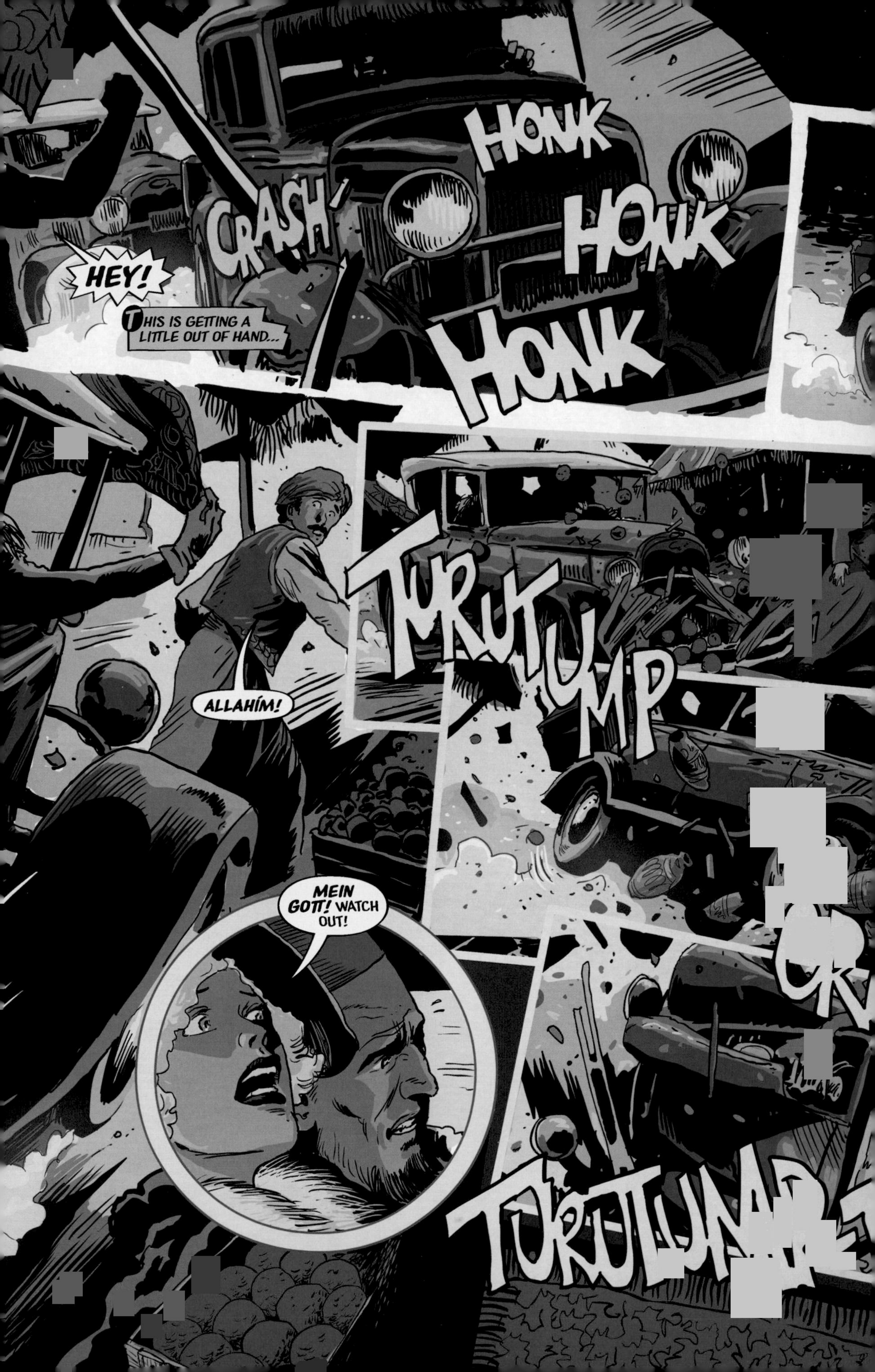
CRASH
HONK
HONK
HONK
HEY!
THIS IS GETTING A LITTLE OUT OF HAND...
TURUTUMP
ALLAHÍM!
MEIN GOTT! WATCH OUT!

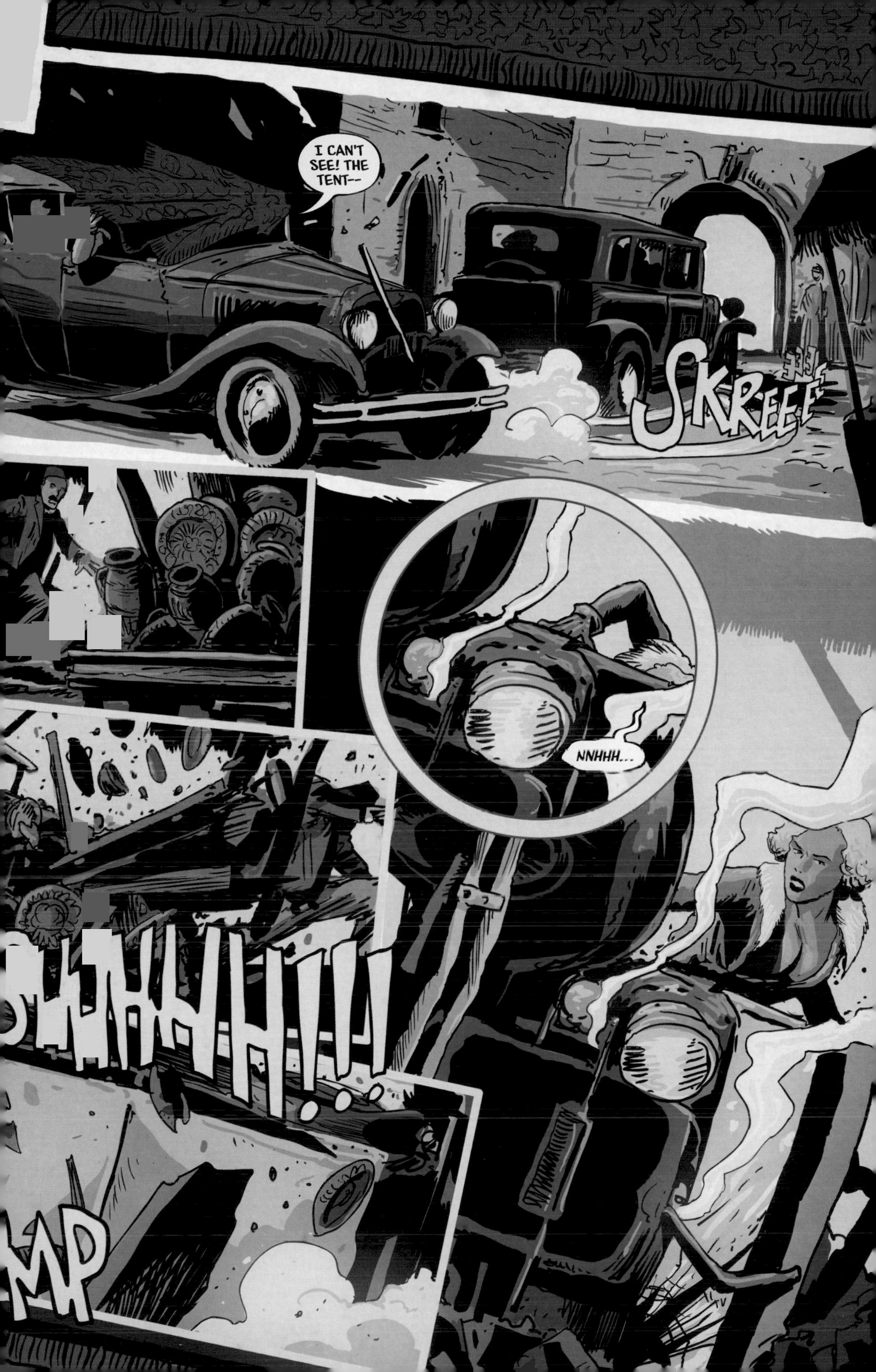
I CAN'T SEE! THE TENT--
SKREEE
NNHHH...

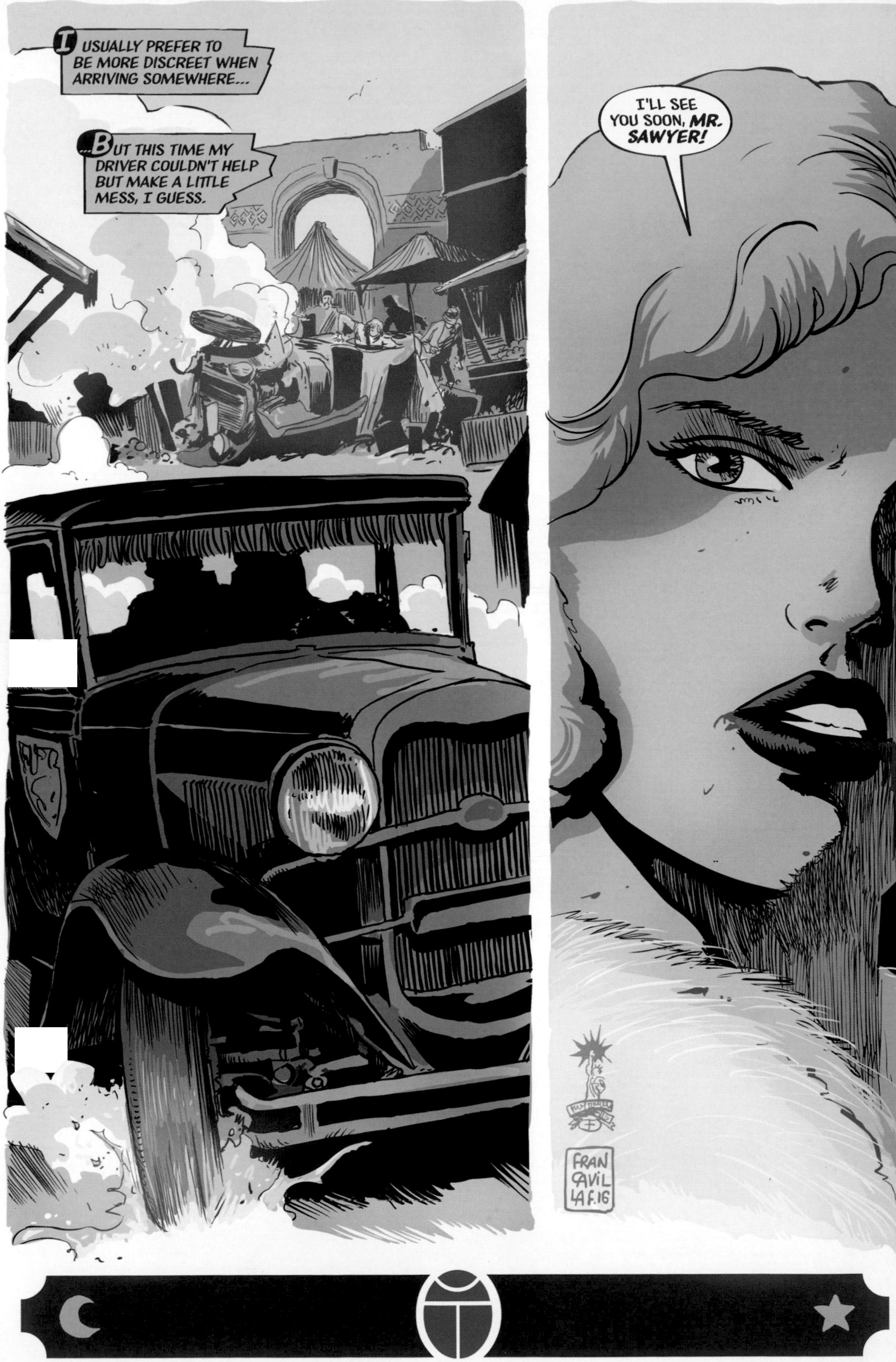
I USUALLY PREFER TO BE MORE DISCREET WHEN ARRIVING SOMEWHERE...
...BUT THIS TIME MY DRIVER COULDN'T HELP BUT MAKE A LITTLE MESS, I GUESS.
I'LL SEE YOU SOON, MR. SAWYER!
FRAN CAVIL LA F.16

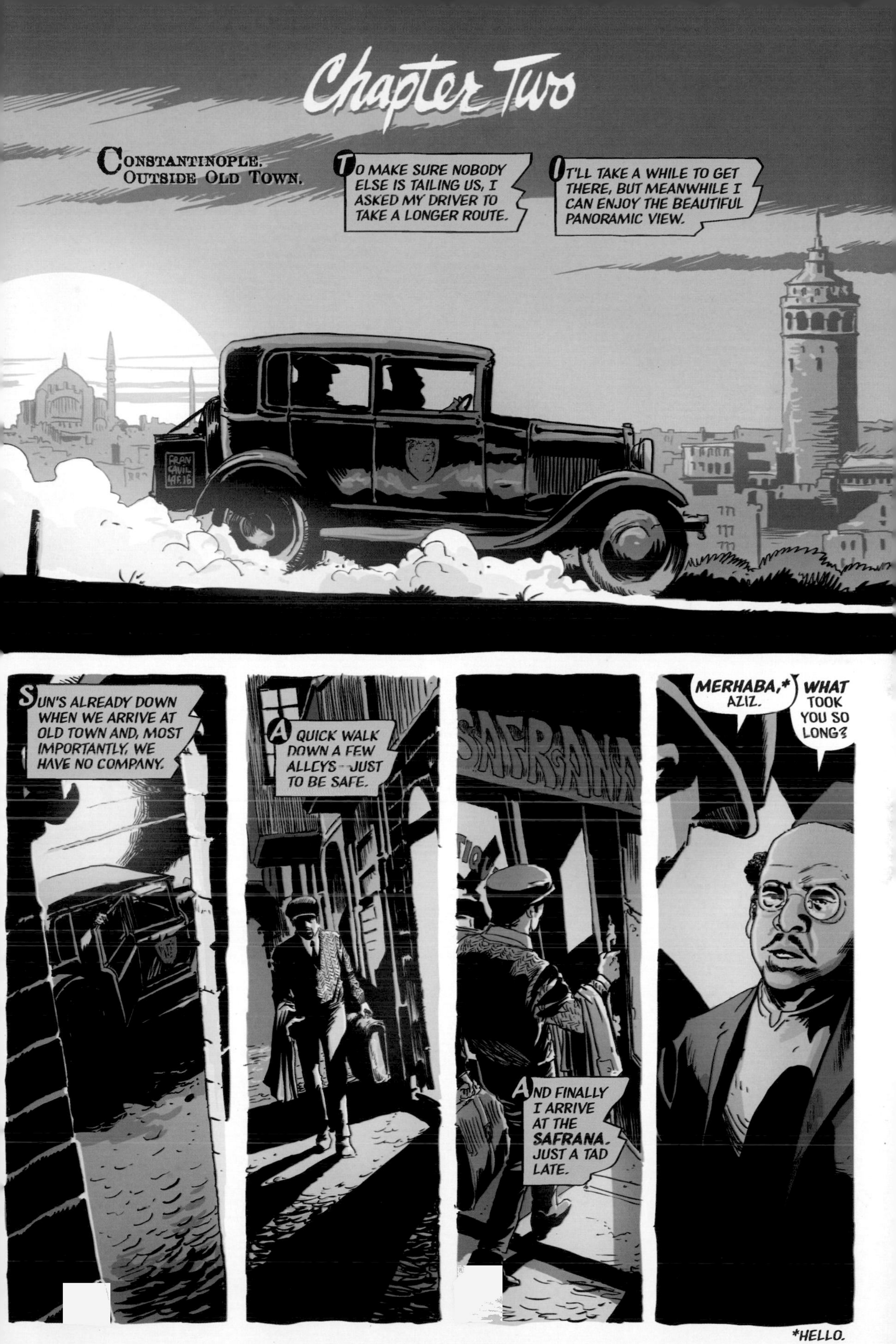
Chapter Two
Constantinople. Outside Old Town.
To make sure nobody else is tailing us, I asked my driver to take a longer route.
It'll take a while to get there, but meanwhile I can enjoy the beautiful panoramic view.
Sun's already down when we arrive at Old Town and, most importantly, we have no company.
A quick walk down a few alleys--just to be safe.
SAFRANA
And finally I arrive at the SAFRANA. Just a tad late.
MERHABA,* AZIZ.
WHAT TOOK YOU SO LONG?

*HELLO.

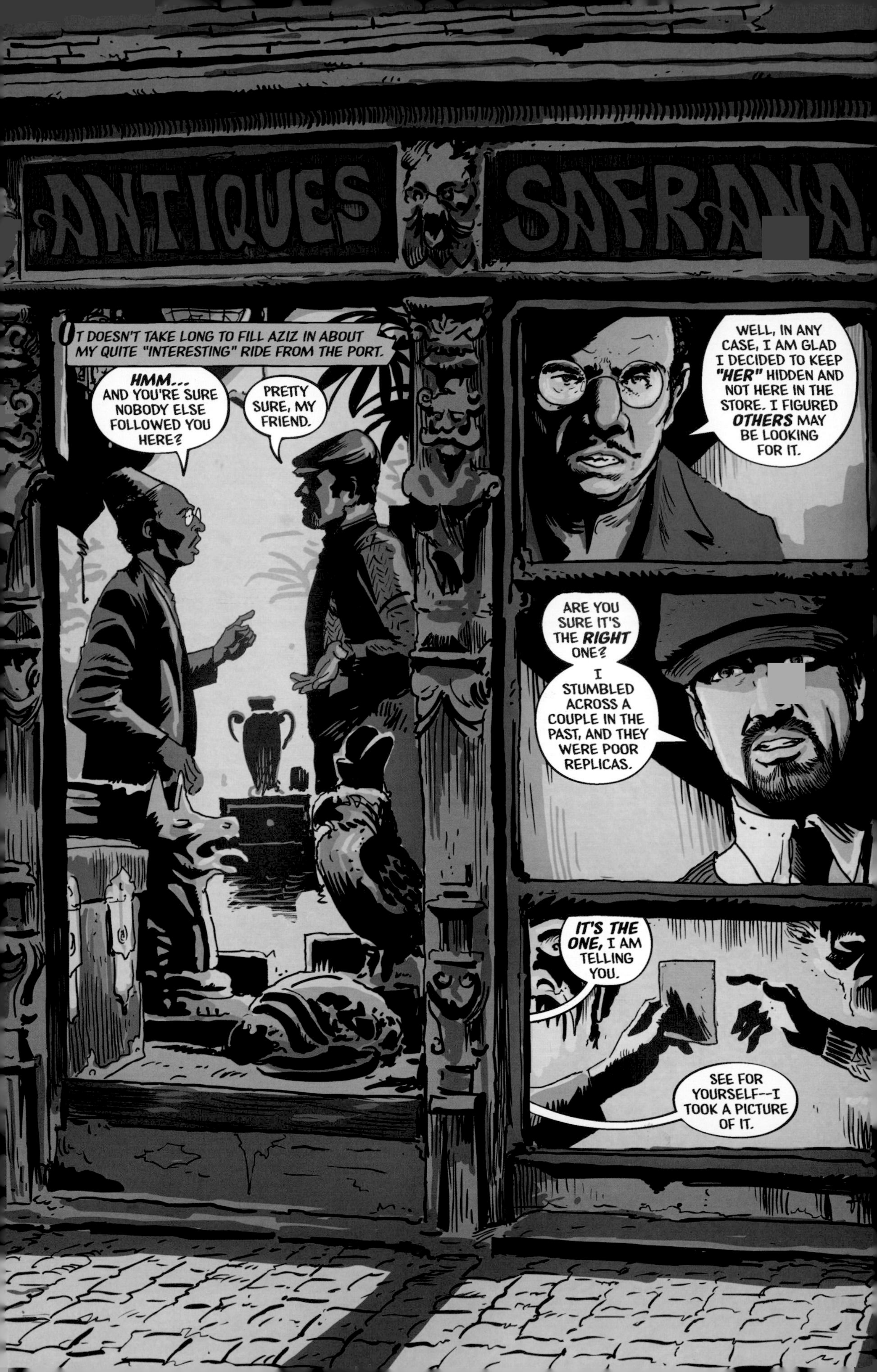
ANTIQUES
SAFRANA
IT DOESN'T TAKE LONG TO FILL AZIZ IN ABOUT MY QUITE "INTERESTING" RIDE FROM THE PORT.
HMM... AND YOU'RE SURE NOBODY ELSE FOLLOWED YOU HERE?
PRETTY SURE, MY FRIEND.
WELL, IN ANY CASE, I AM GLAD I DECIDED TO KEEP "HER" HIDDEN AND NOT HERE IN THE STORE. I FIGURED OTHERS MAY BE LOOKING FOR IT.
ARE YOU SURE IT'S THE RIGHT ONE?
I STUMBLED ACROSS A COUPLE IN THE PAST, AND THEY WERE POOR REPLICAS.
IT'S THE ONE, I AM TELLING YOU.
SEE FOR YOURSELF--I TOOK A PICTURE OF IT.

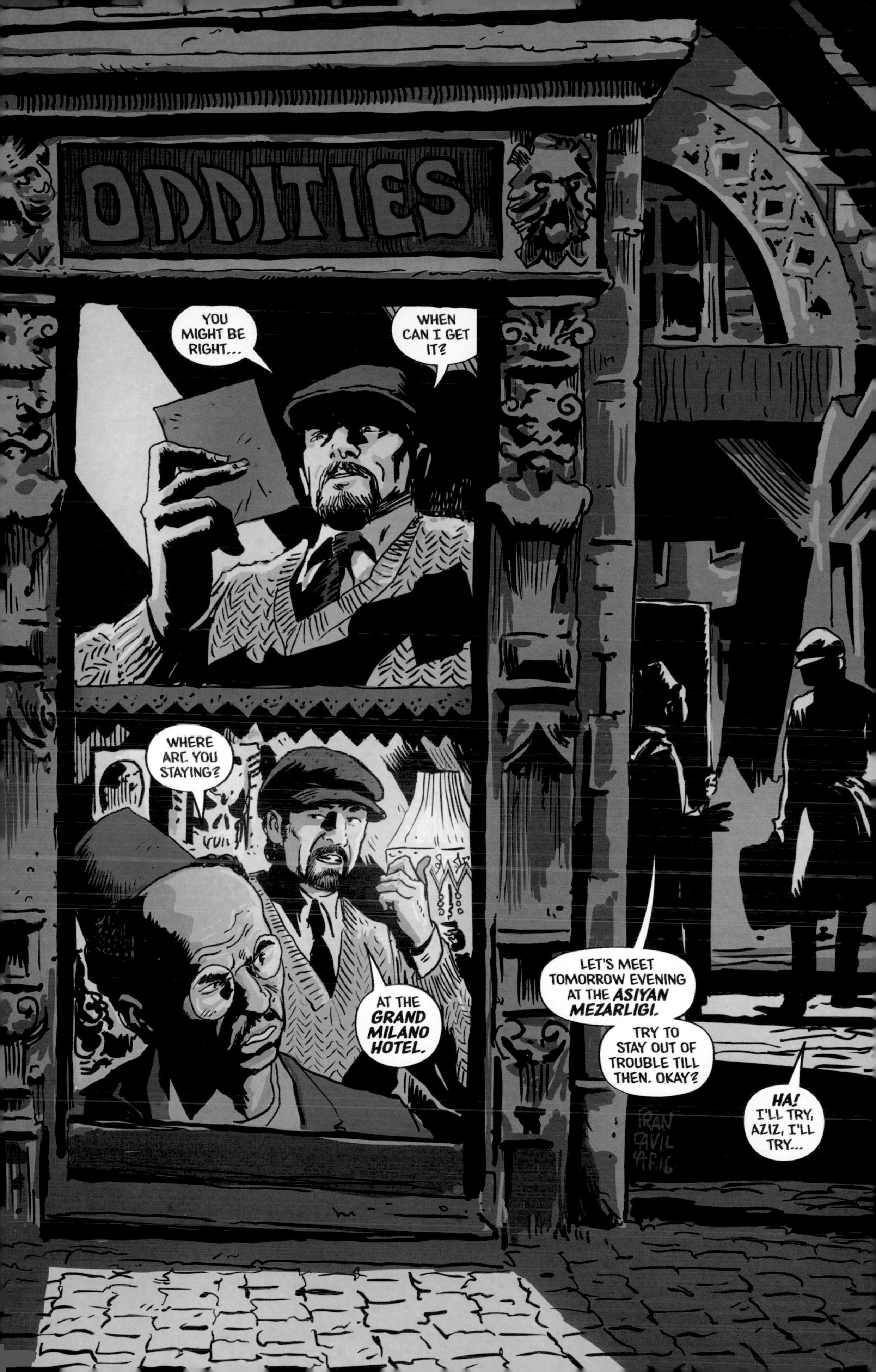
ODDITIES
YOU MIGHT BE RIGHT...
WHEN CAN I GET IT?
WHERE ARE YOU STAYING?
AT THE GRAND MILANO HOTEL.
LET'S MEET TOMORROW EVENING AT THE ASIYAN MEZARLIGI.
TRY TO STAY OUT OF TROUBLE TILL THEN. OKAY?
HA! I'LL TRY, AZIZ, I'LL TRY...
FRAN GAVIL 14.F.16

AAHHRRGGHH
AAAAGHH

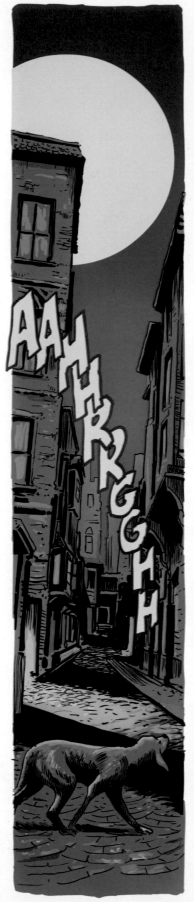

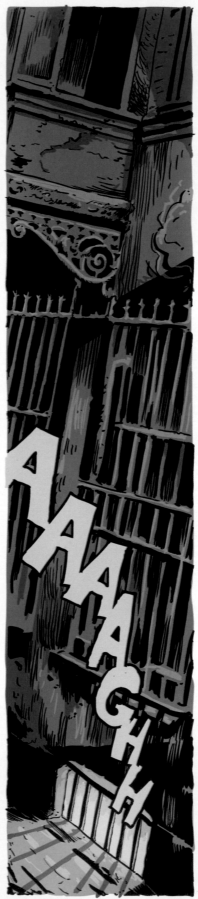

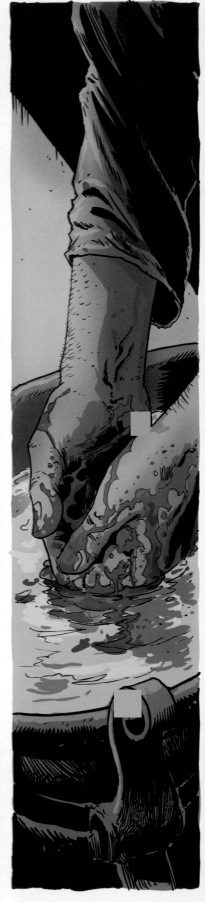

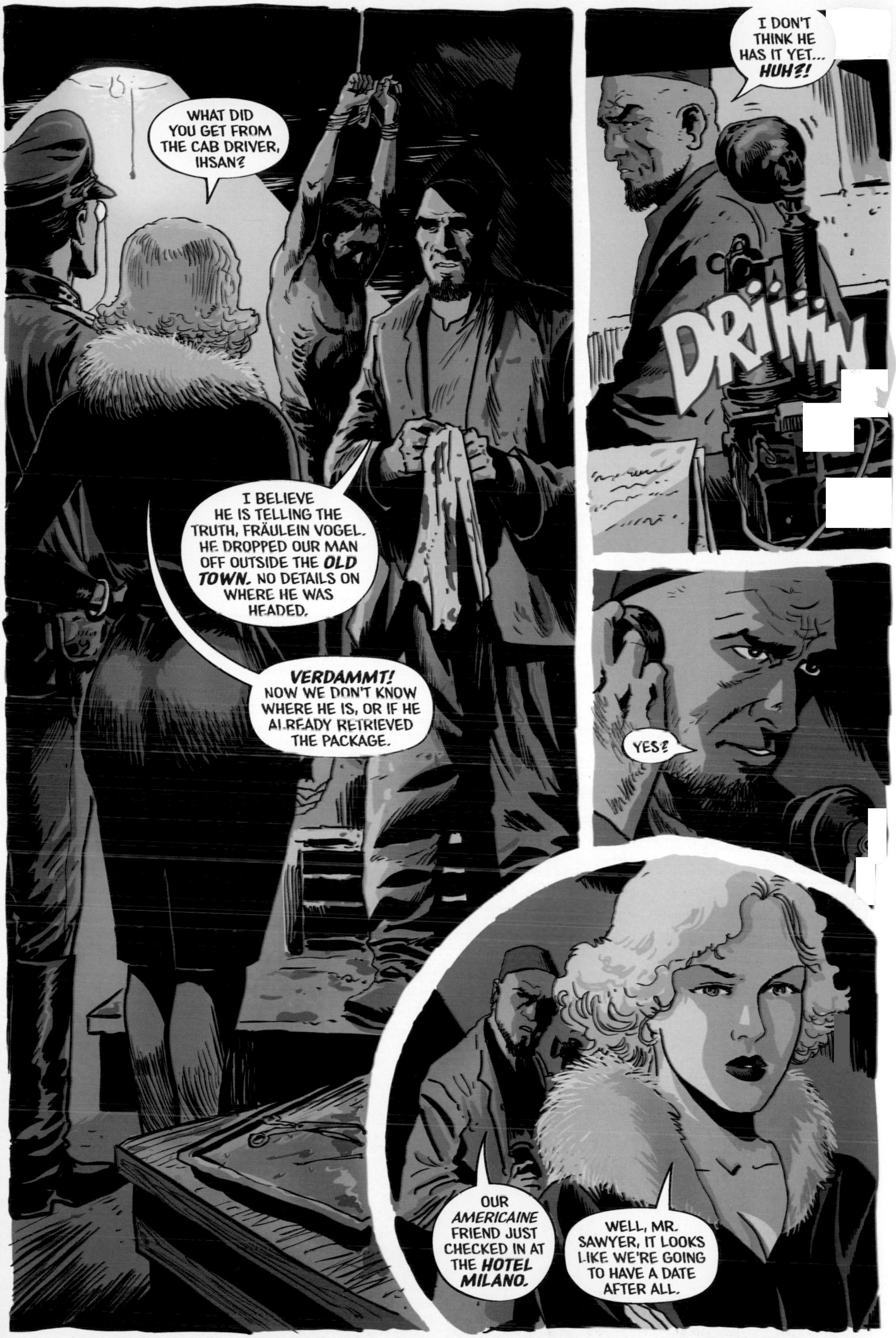
WHAT DID YOU GET FROM THE CAB DRIVER, IHSAN?
I BELIEVE HE IS TELLING THE TRUTH, FRÄULEIN VOGEL. HE DROPPED OUR MAN OFF OUTSIDE THE OLD TOWN. NO DETAILS ON WHERE HE WAS HEADED.
VERDAMMT! NOW WE DON'T KNOW WHERE HE IS, OR IF HE ALREADY RETRIEVED THE PACKAGE.
I DON'T THINK HE HAS IT YET... HUH?!
DRIIIIN
YES?
OUR AMERICAINE FRIEND JUST CHECKED IN AT THE HOTEL MILANO.
WELL, MR. SAWYER, IT LOOKS LIKE WE'RE GOING TO HAVE A DATE AFTER ALL.

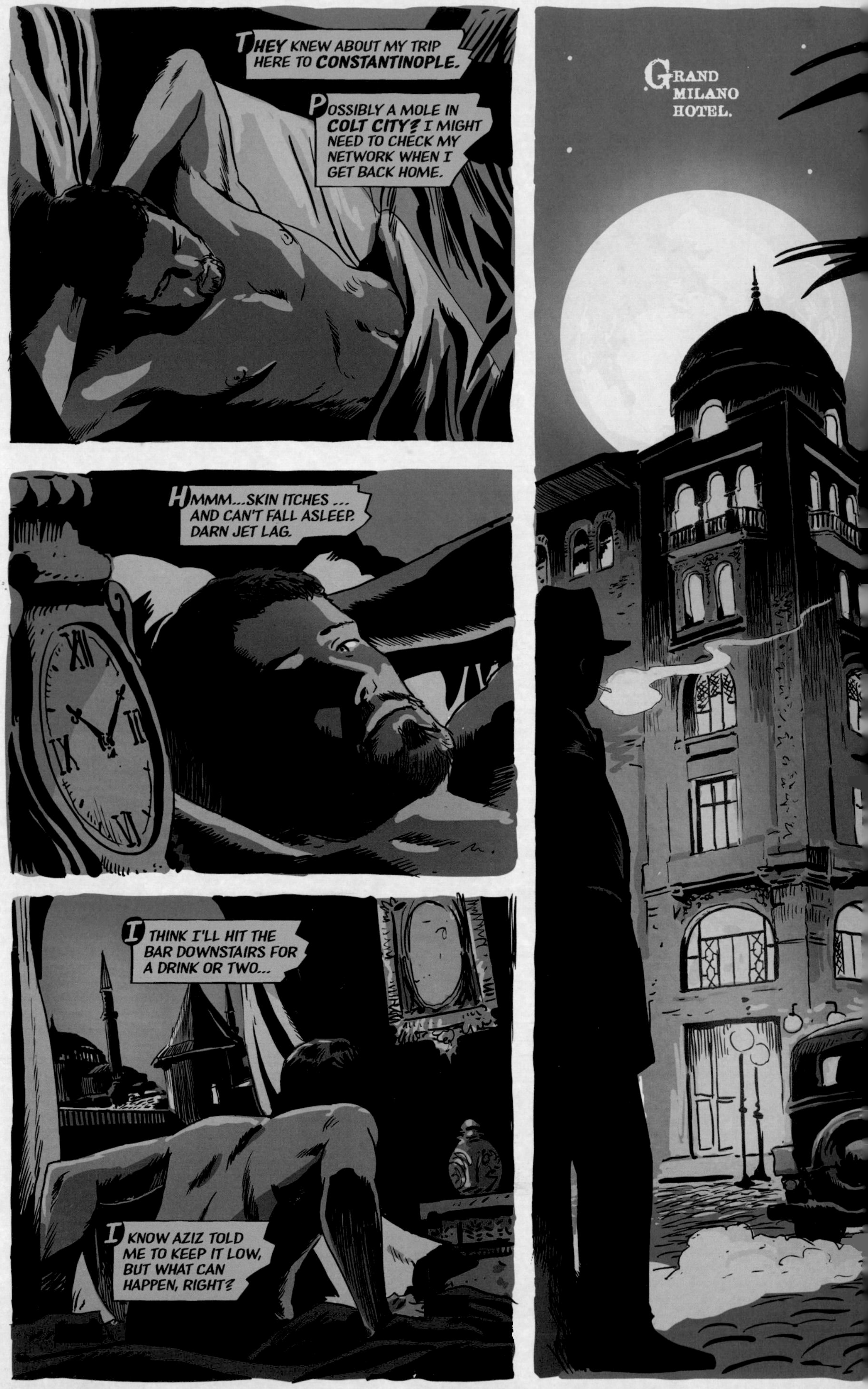
THEY KNEW ABOUT MY TRIP HERE TO CONSTANTINOPLE.
POSSIBLY A MOLE IN COLT CITY? I MIGHT NEED TO CHECK MY NETWORK WHEN I GET BACK HOME.
HMMM...SKIN ITCHES ... AND CAN'T FALL ASLEEP. DARN JET LAG.
I THINK I'LL HIT THE BAR DOWNSTAIRS FOR A DRINK OR TWO...
I KNOW AZIZ TOLD ME TO KEEP IT LOW, BUT WHAT CAN HAPPEN, RIGHT?
GRAND MILANO HOTEL.

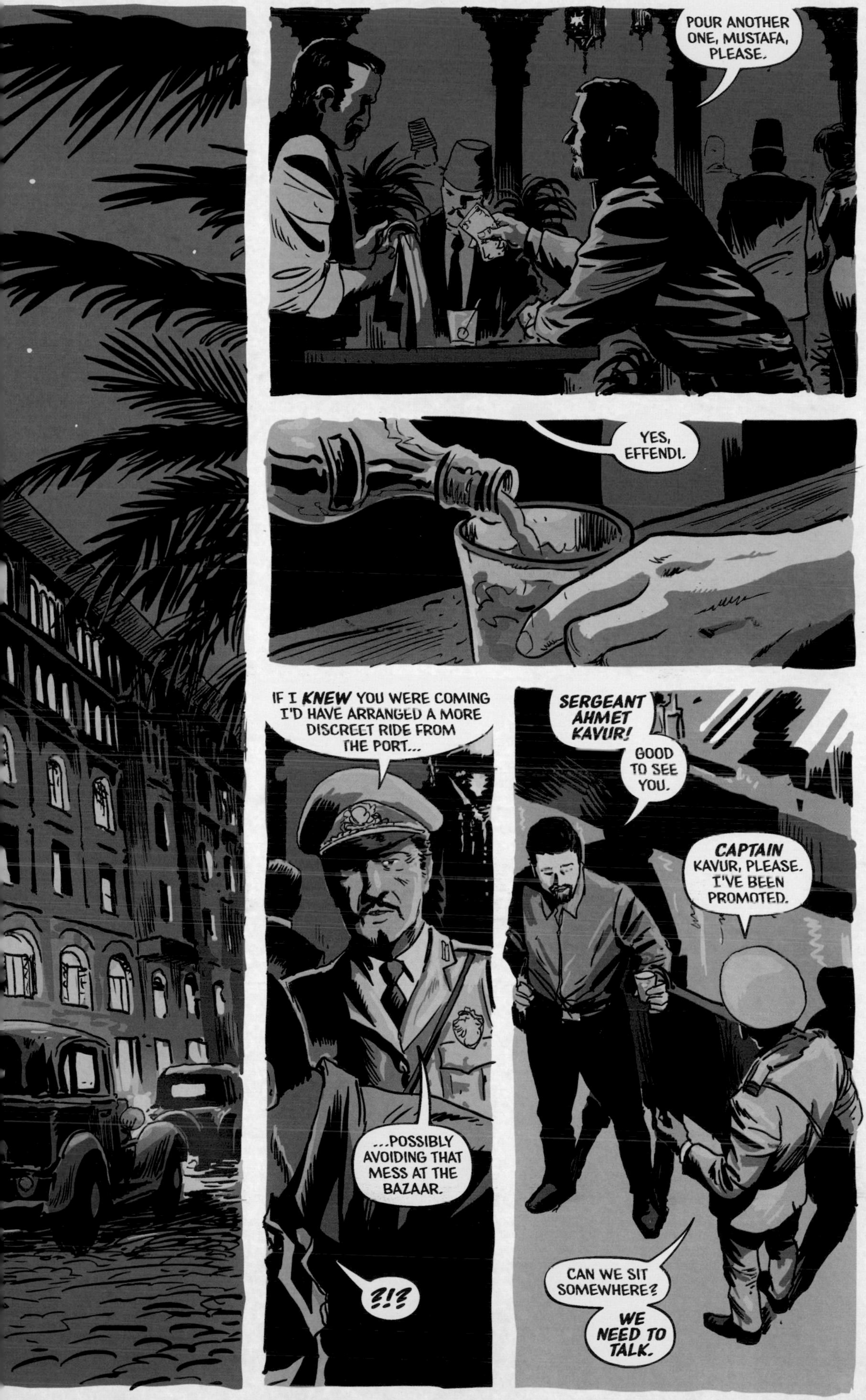
POUR ANOTHER ONE, MUSTAFA, PLEASE.
YES, EFFENDI.
IF I *KNEW* YOU WERE COMING I'D HAVE ARRANGED A MORE DISCREET RIDE FROM THE PORT...
...POSSIBLY AVOIDING THAT MESS AT THE BAZAAR.
?!?
SERGEANT AHMET KAVUR!
GOOD TO SEE YOU.
CAPTAIN KAVUR, PLEASE. I'VE BEEN PROMOTED.
CAN WE SIT SOMEWHERE?
WE NEED TO TALK.

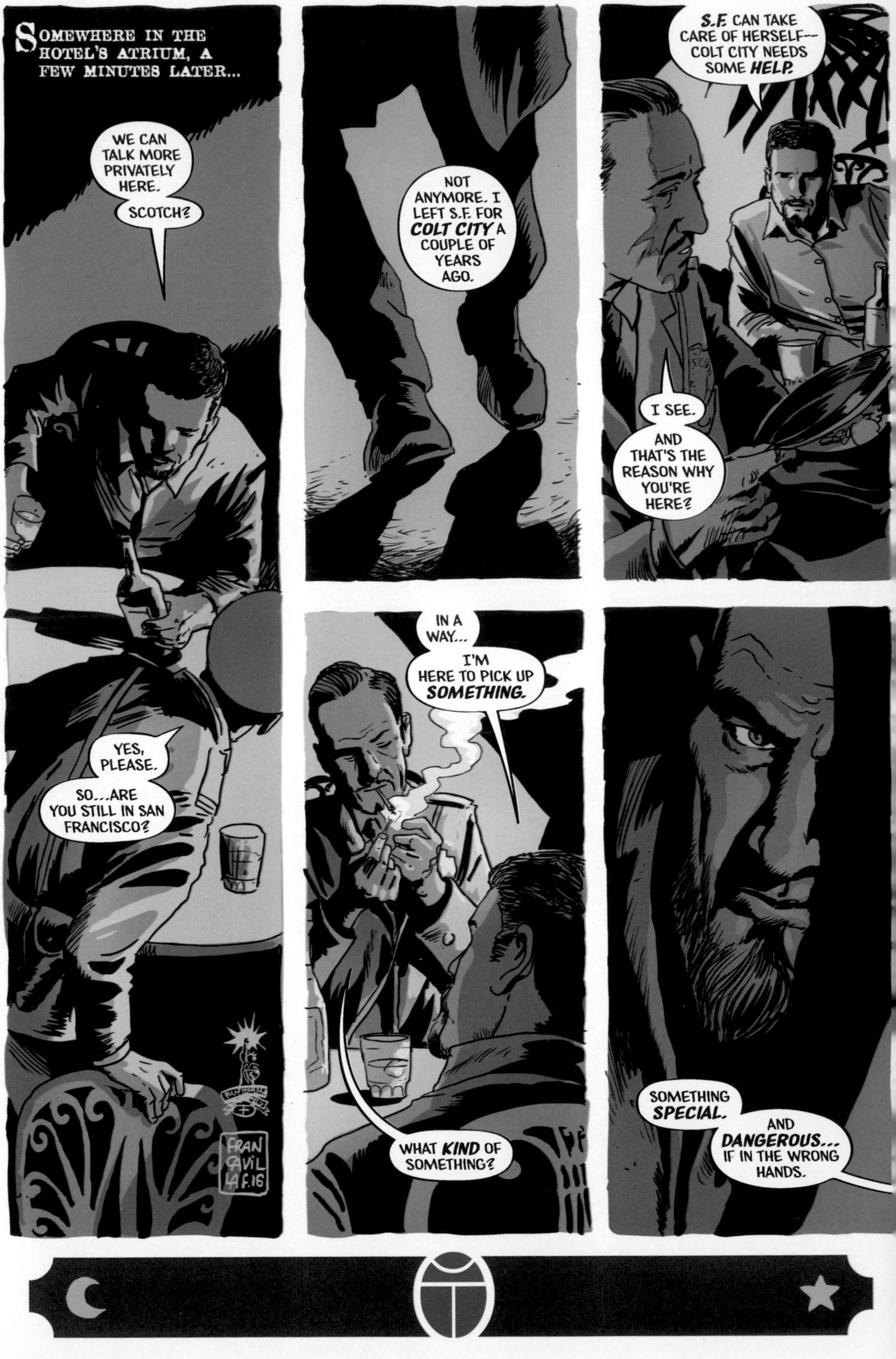
SOMEWHERE IN THE HOTEL'S ATRIUM, A FEW MINUTES LATER...
WE CAN TALK MORE PRIVATELY HERE.
SCOTCH?
NOT ANYMORE. I LEFT S.F. FOR COLT CITY A COUPLE OF YEARS AGO.
S.F. CAN TAKE CARE OF HERSELF-- COLT CITY NEEDS SOME HELP.
I SEE.
AND THAT'S THE REASON WHY YOU'RE HERE?
YES, PLEASE.
SO...ARE YOU STILL IN SAN FRANCISCO?
IN A WAY...
I'M HERE TO PICK UP SOMETHING.
WHAT KIND OF SOMETHING?
SOMETHING SPECIAL.
AND DANGEROUS... IF IN THE WRONG HANDS.
FRANCAVILLA F.16

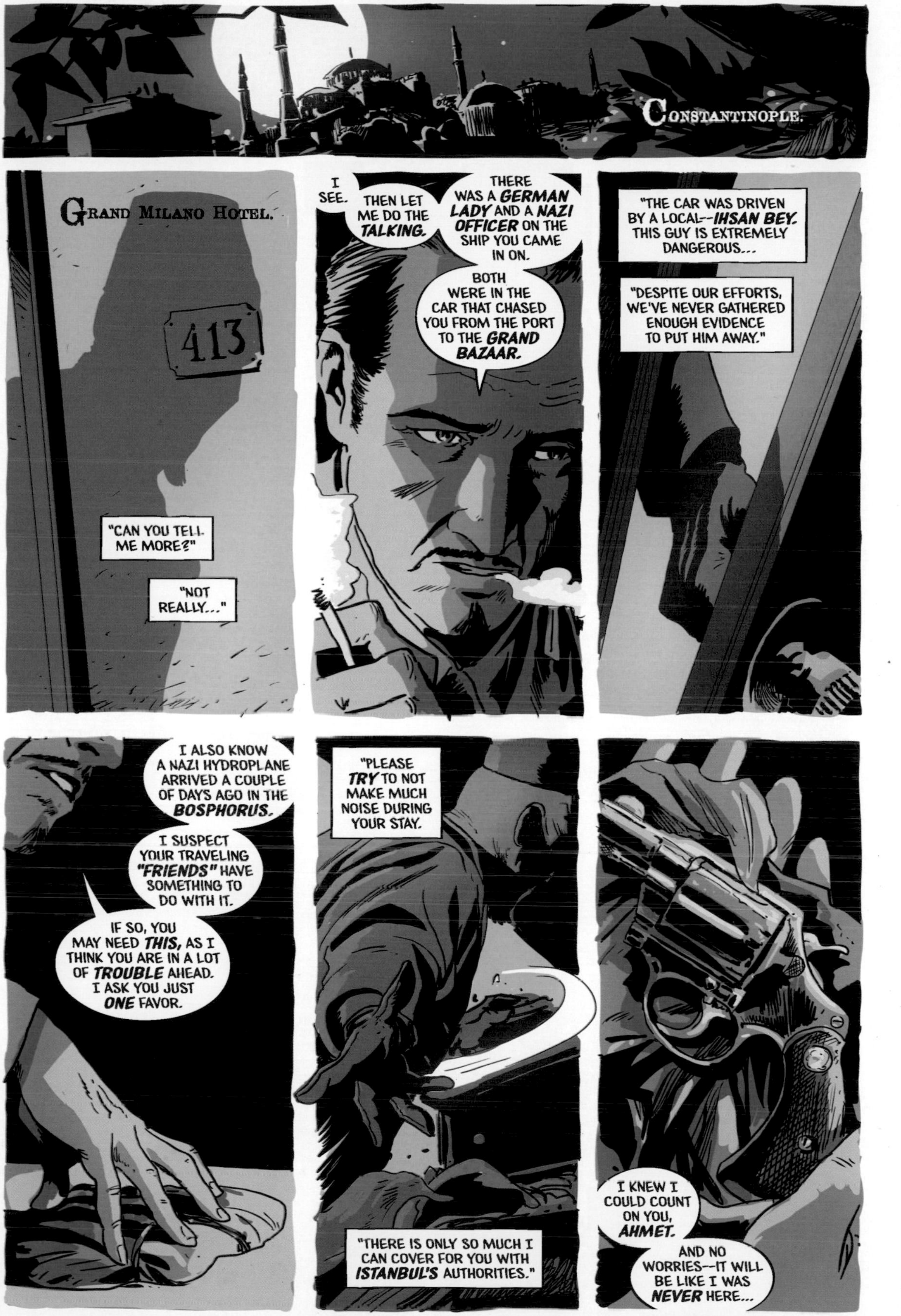

CONSTANTINOPLE.
GRAND MILANO HOTEL.
413
"CAN YOU TELL ME MORE?"
"NOT REALLY..."
I SEE.
THEN LET ME DO THE TALKING.
THERE WAS A GERMAN LADY AND A NAZI OFFICER ON THE SHIP YOU CAME IN ON.
BOTH WERE IN THE CAR THAT CHASED YOU FROM THE PORT TO THE GRAND BAZAAR.
"THE CAR WAS DRIVEN BY A LOCAL--IHSAN BEY. THIS GUY IS EXTREMELY DANGEROUS...
"DESPITE OUR EFFORTS, WE'VE NEVER GATHERED ENOUGH EVIDENCE TO PUT HIM AWAY."
I ALSO KNOW A NAZI HYDROPLANE ARRIVED A COUPLE OF DAYS AGO IN THE BOSPHORUS.
I SUSPECT YOUR TRAVELING "FRIENDS" HAVE SOMETHING TO DO WITH IT.
IF SO, YOU MAY NEED THIS, AS I THINK YOU ARE IN A LOT OF TROUBLE AHEAD. I ASK YOU JUST ONE FAVOR.
"PLEASE TRY TO NOT MAKE MUCH NOISE DURING YOUR STAY.
"THERE IS ONLY SO MUCH I CAN COVER FOR YOU WITH ISTANBUL'S AUTHORITIES."
I KNEW I COULD COUNT ON YOU, AHMET.
AND NO WORRIES--IT WILL BE LIKE I WAS NEVER HERE...

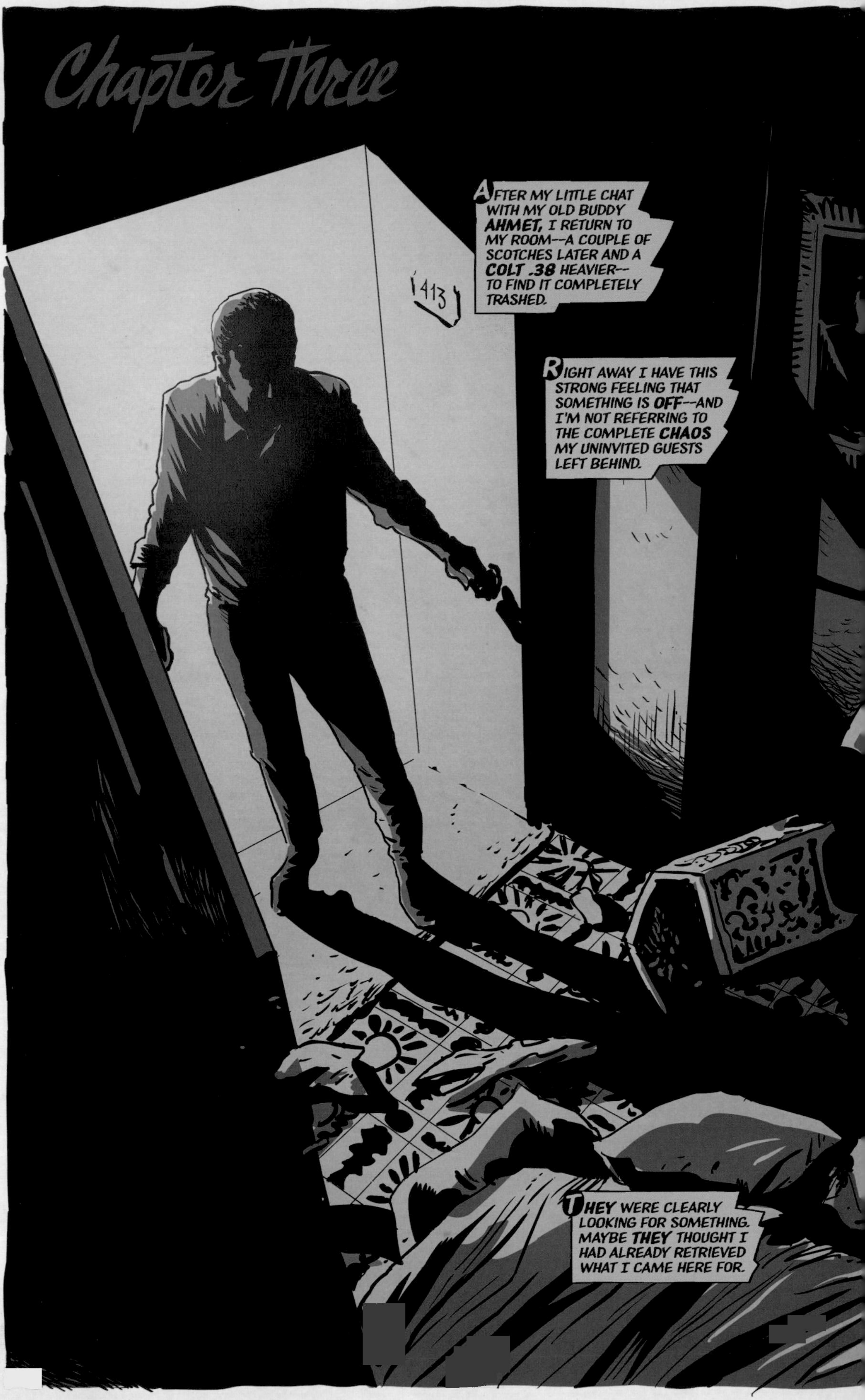
Chapter Three
413
AFTER MY LITTLE CHAT WITH MY OLD BUDDY AHMET, I RETURN TO MY ROOM--A COUPLE OF SCOTCHES LATER AND A COLT .38 HEAVIER--TO FIND IT COMPLETELY TRASHED.
RIGHT AWAY I HAVE THIS STRONG FEELING THAT SOMETHING IS OFF--AND I'M NOT REFERRING TO THE COMPLETE CHAOS MY UNINVITED GUESTS LEFT BEHIND.
THEY WERE CLEARLY LOOKING FOR SOMETHING. MAYBE THEY THOUGHT I HAD ALREADY RETRIEVED WHAT I CAME HERE FOR.

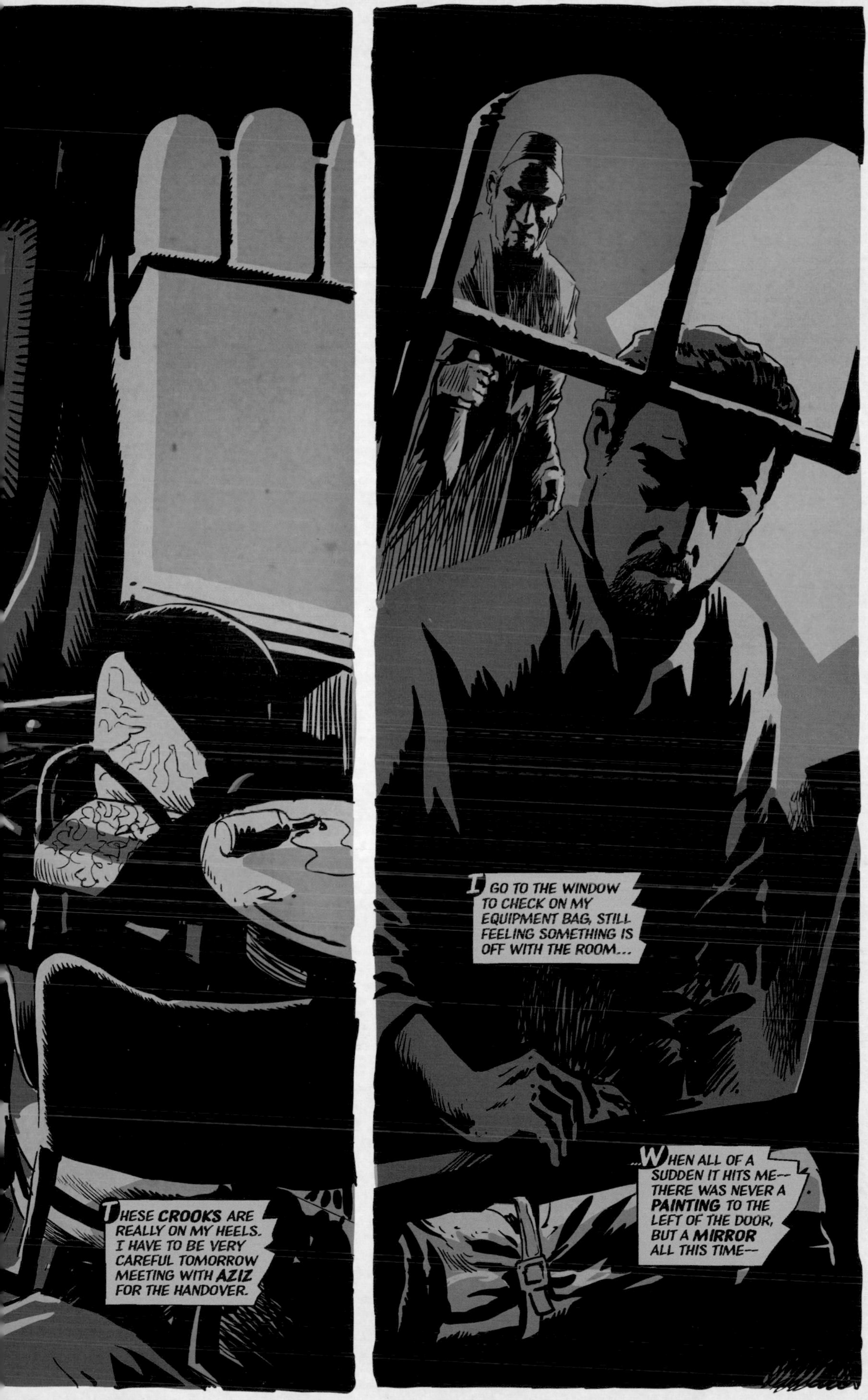
THESE CROOKS ARE REALLY ON MY HEELS. I HAVE TO BE VERY CAREFUL TOMORROW MEETING WITH AZIZ FOR THE HANDOVER.
I GO TO THE WINDOW TO CHECK ON MY EQUIPMENT BAG, STILL FEELING SOMETHING IS OFF WITH THE ROOM...
...WHEN ALL OF A SUDDEN IT HITS ME-- THERE WAS NEVER A PAINTING TO THE LEFT OF THE DOOR, BUT A MIRROR ALL THIS TIME--

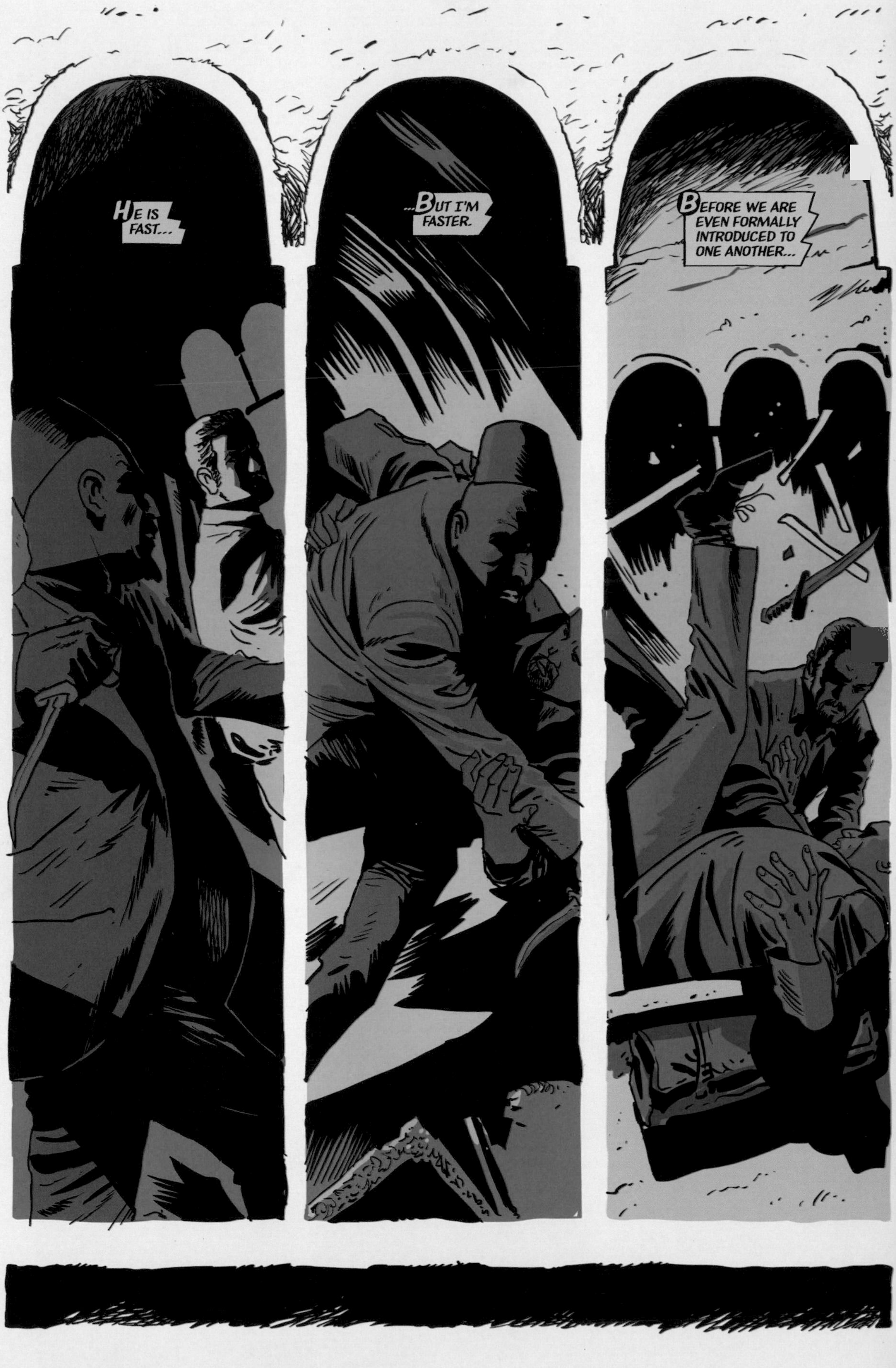
HE IS FAST...
...BUT I'M FASTER.
BEFORE WE ARE EVEN FORMALLY INTRODUCED TO ONE ANOTHER...

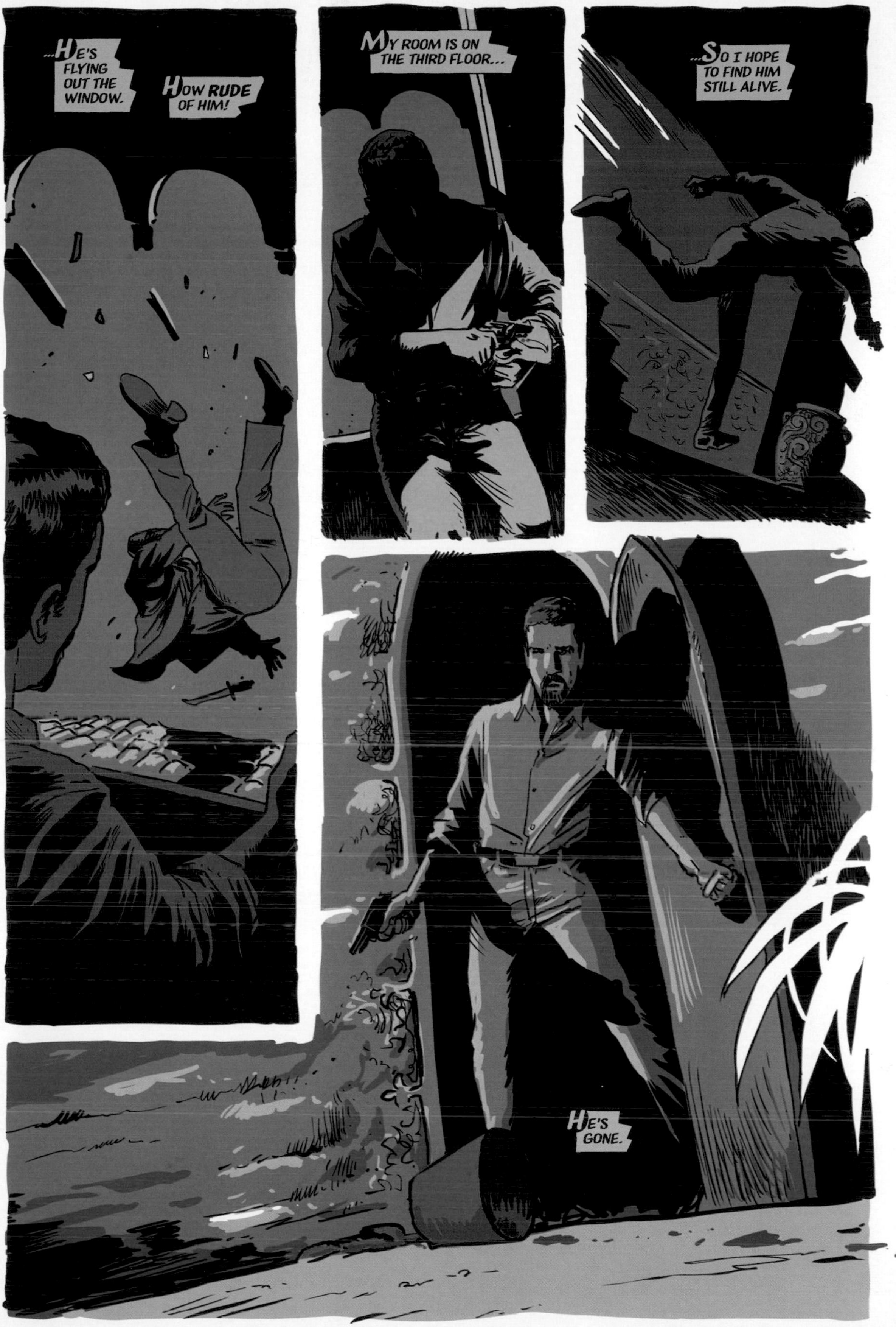
...HE'S FLYING OUT THE WINDOW.
HOW RUDE OF HIM!
MY ROOM IS ON THE THIRD FLOOR...
...SO I HOPE TO FIND HIM STILL ALIVE.
HE'S GONE.

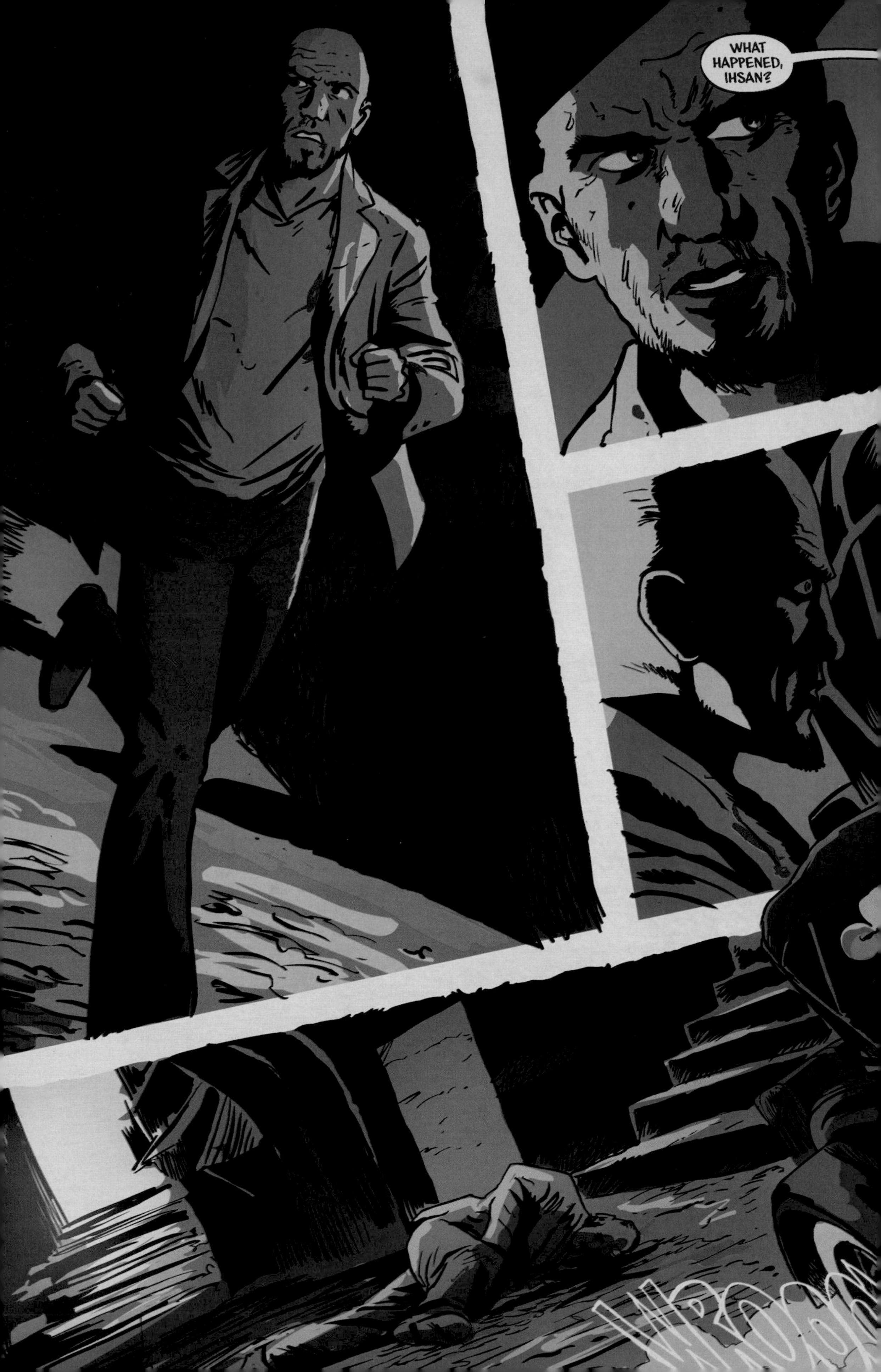
WHAT HAPPENED, IHSAN?

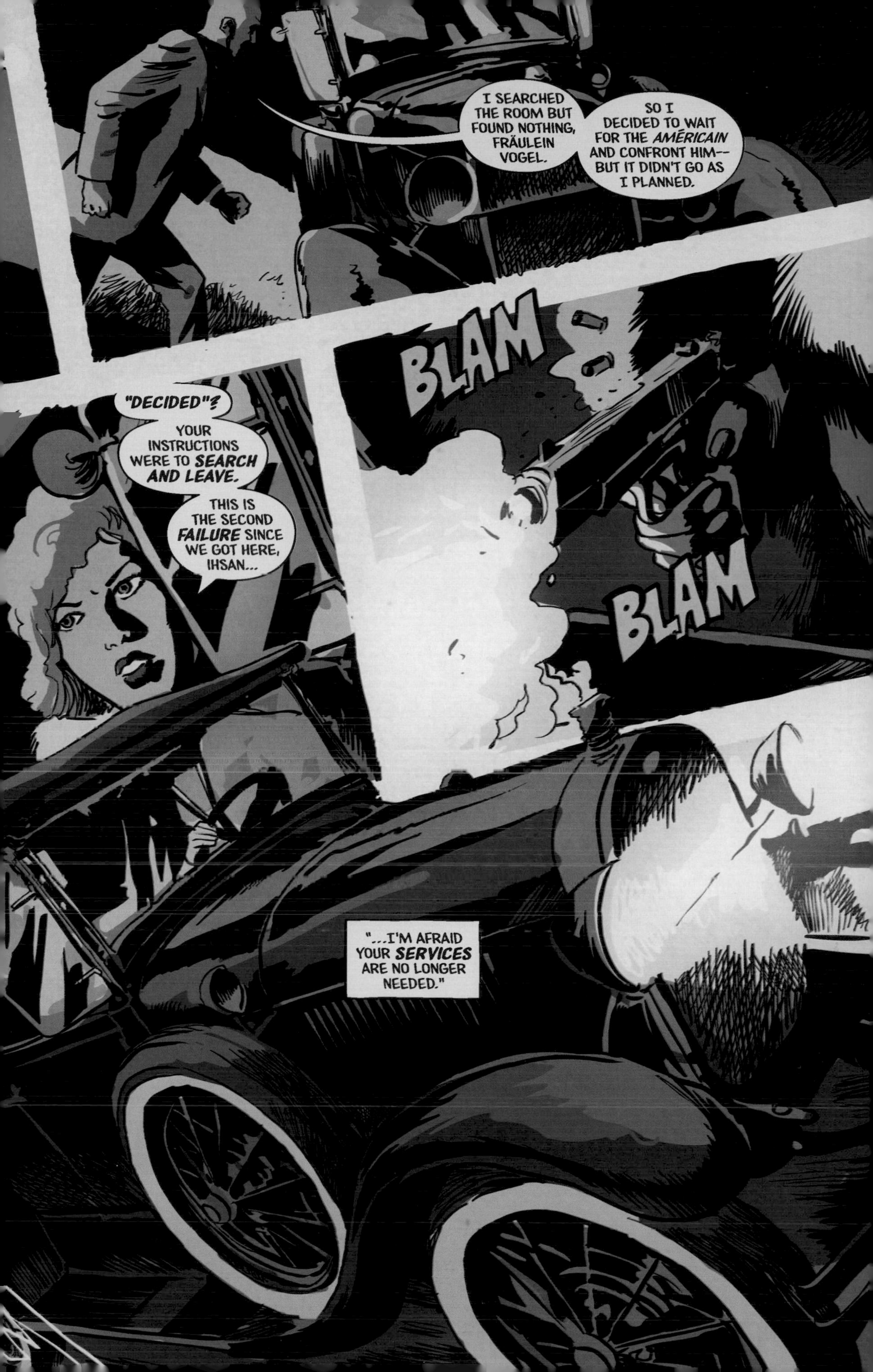

I SEARCHED THE ROOM BUT FOUND NOTHING, FRÄULEIN VOGEL.
SO I DECIDED TO WAIT FOR THE *AMÉRICAIN* AND CONFRONT HIM-- BUT IT DIDN'T GO AS I PLANNED.
"DECIDED"?
YOUR INSTRUCTIONS WERE TO *SEARCH AND LEAVE.*
THIS IS THE SECOND *FAILURE* SINCE WE GOT HERE, IHSAN...
BLAM
BLAM
"...I'M AFRAID YOUR *SERVICES* ARE NO LONGER NEEDED."

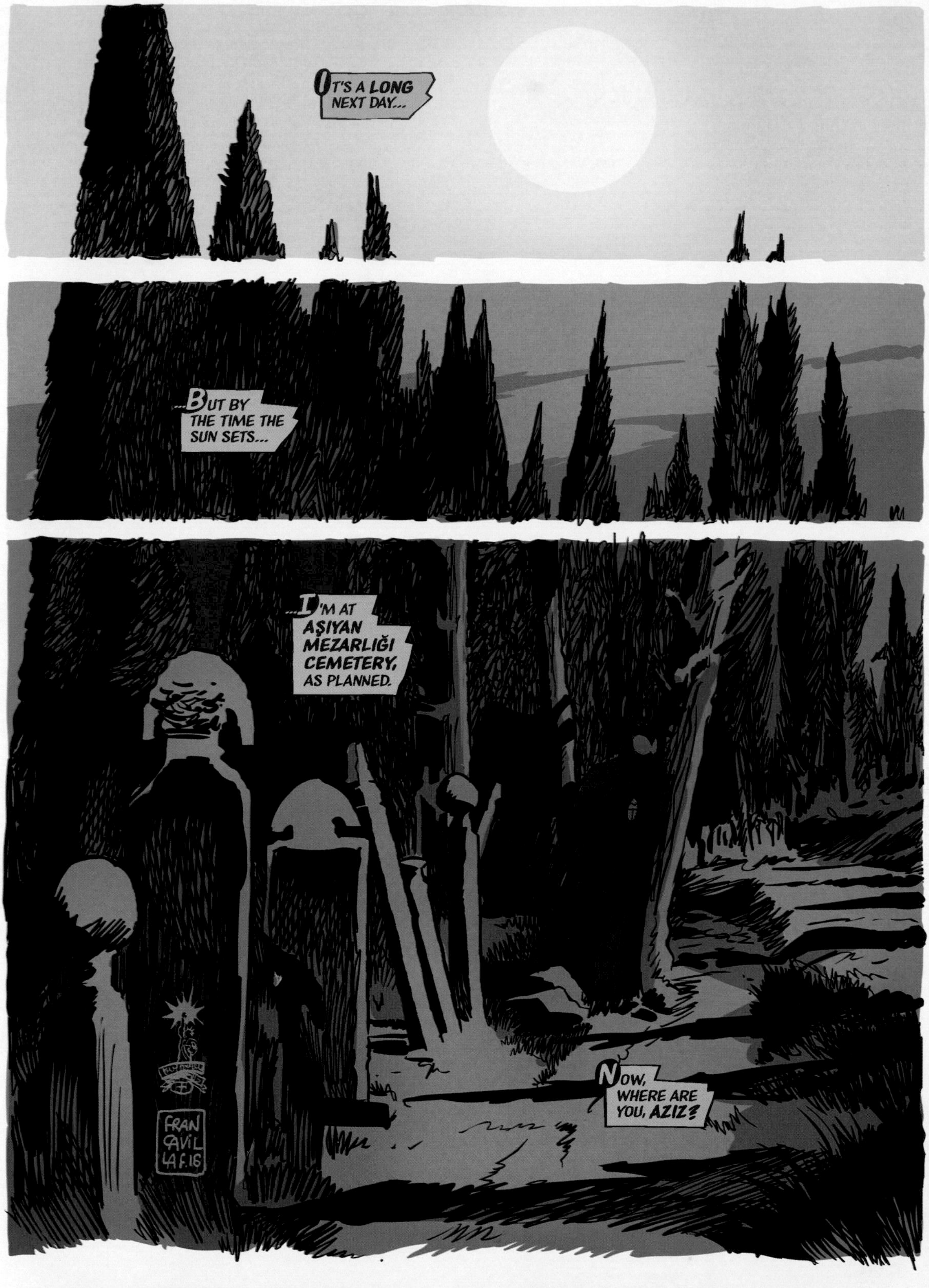
IT'S A LONG NEXT DAY...
...BUT BY THE TIME THE SUN SETS...
...I'M AT AŞIYAN MEZARLIĞI CEMETERY, AS PLANNED.
NOW, WHERE ARE YOU, AZIZ?
FRAN CAVIL LA F.16

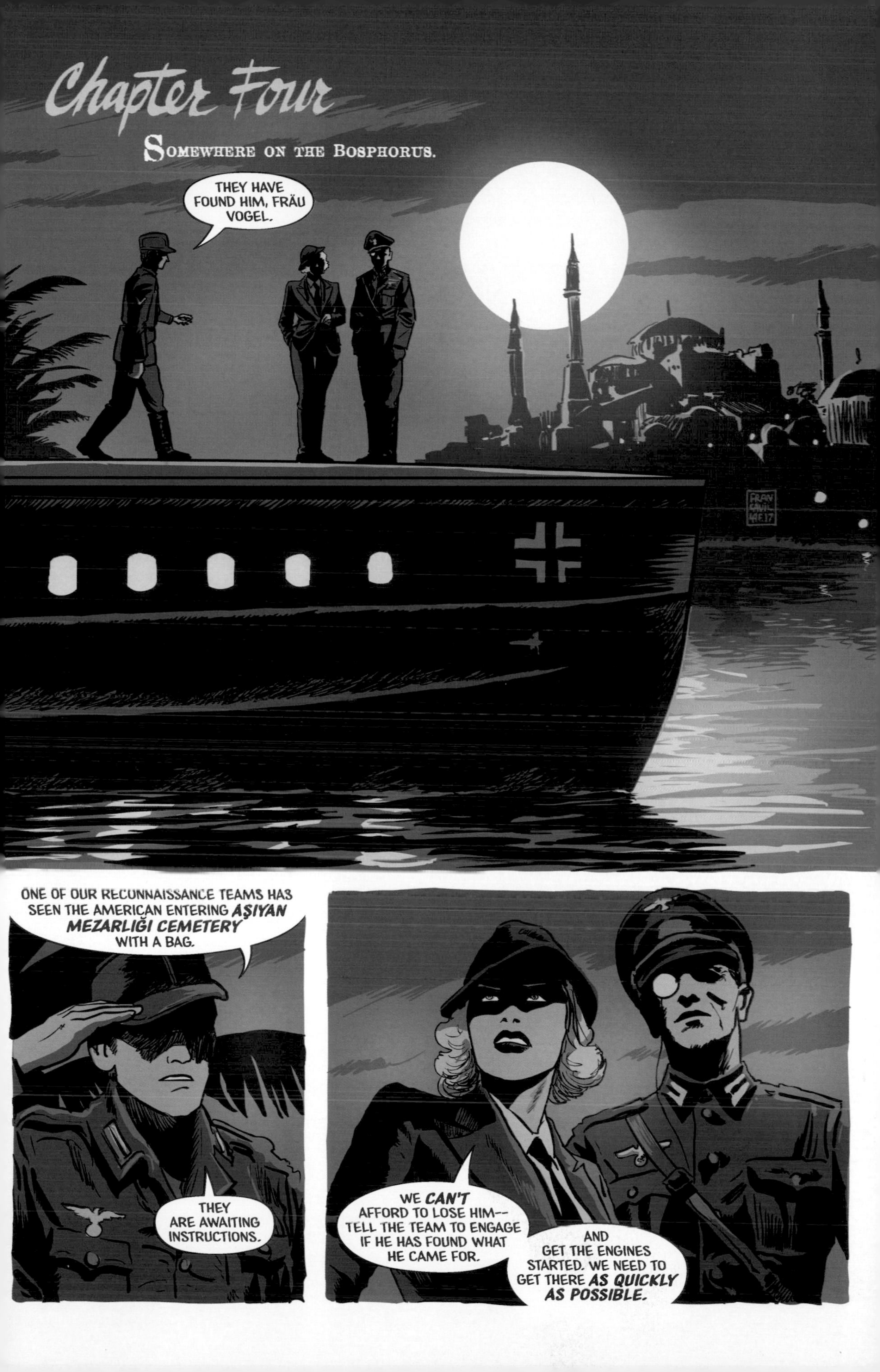
Chapter Four
Somewhere on the Bosphorus.
THEY HAVE FOUND HIM, FRÄU VOGEL.
FRAN CAVILLIE 17
ONE OF OUR RECONNAISSANCE TEAMS HAS SEEN THE AMERICAN ENTERING AŞIYAN MEZARLIĞI CEMETERY WITH A BAG.
THEY ARE AWAITING INSTRUCTIONS.
WE CAN'T AFFORD TO LOSE HIM-- TELL THE TEAM TO ENGAGE IF HE HAS FOUND WHAT HE CAME FOR.
AND GET THE ENGINES STARTED. WE NEED TO GET THERE AS QUICKLY AS POSSIBLE.

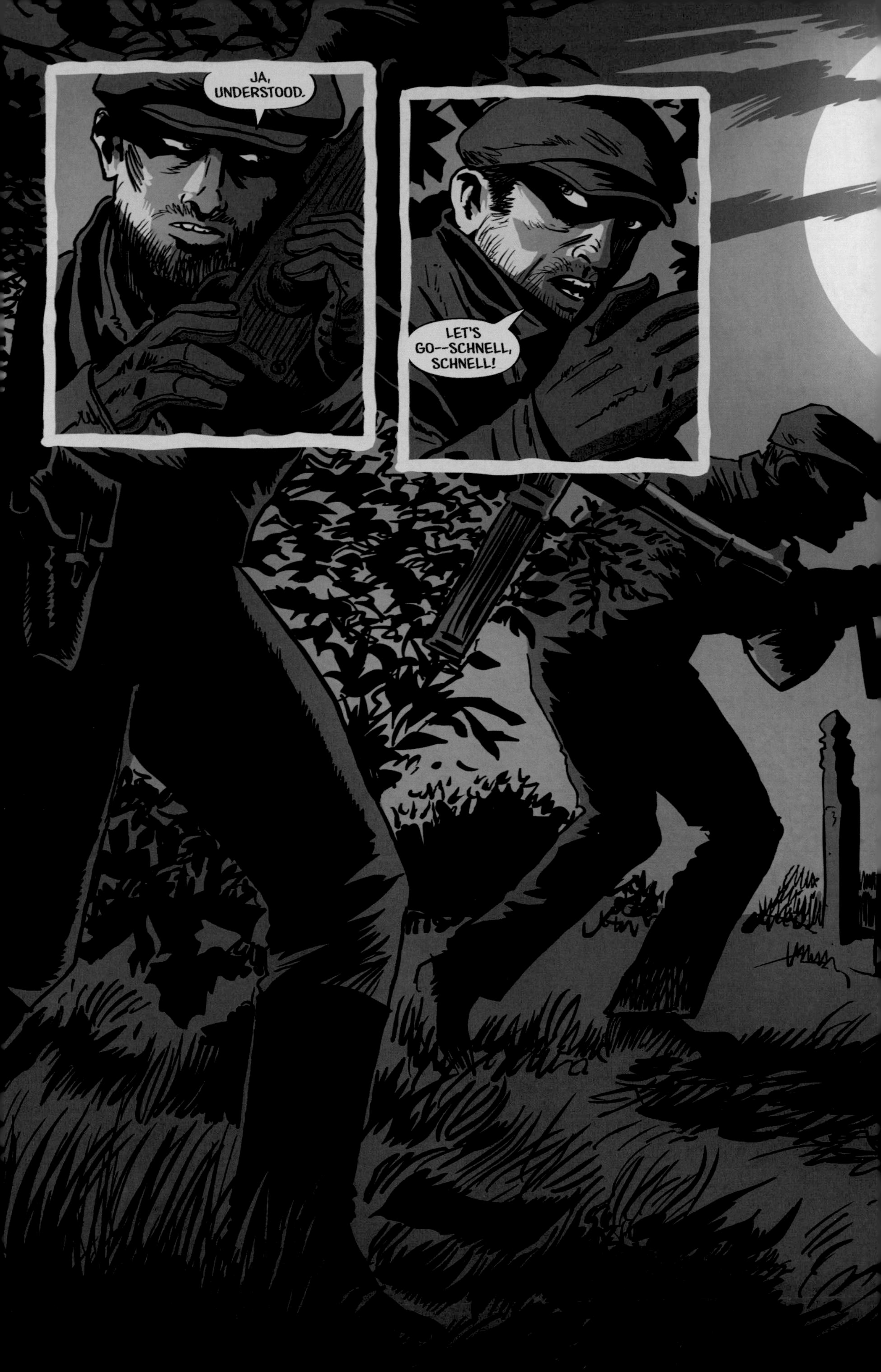
JA, UNDERSTOOD.
LET'S GO--SCHNELL, SCHNELL!

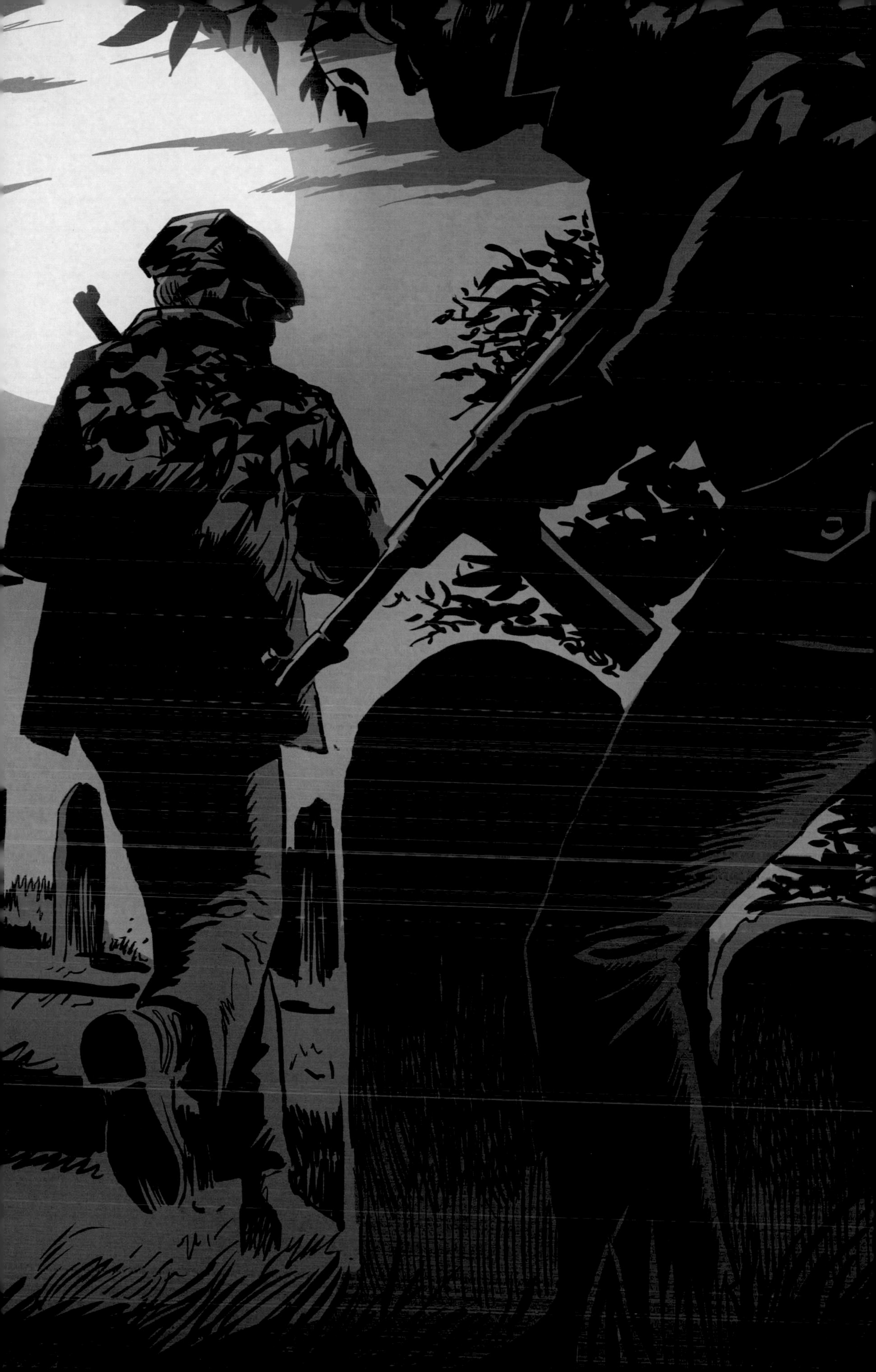

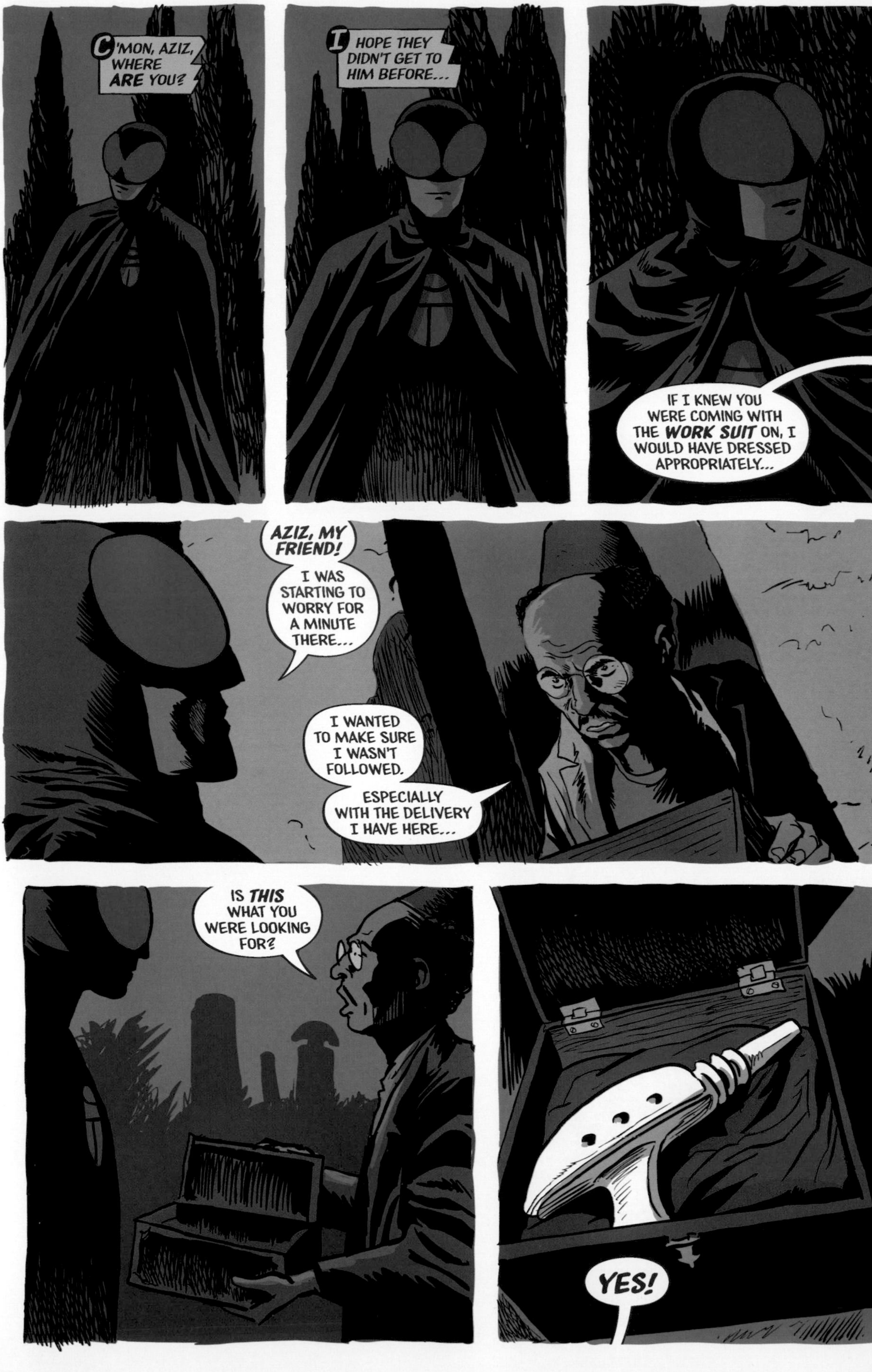
C'MON, AZIZ, WHERE ARE YOU?
I HOPE THEY DIDN'T GET TO HIM BEFORE...
IF I KNEW YOU WERE COMING WITH THE WORK SUIT ON, I WOULD HAVE DRESSED APPROPRIATELY...
AZIZ, MY FRIEND!
I WAS STARTING TO WORRY FOR A MINUTE THERE...
I WANTED TO MAKE SURE I WASN'T FOLLOWED.
ESPECIALLY WITH THE DELIVERY I HAVE HERE...
IS THIS WHAT YOU WERE LOOKING FOR?
YES!

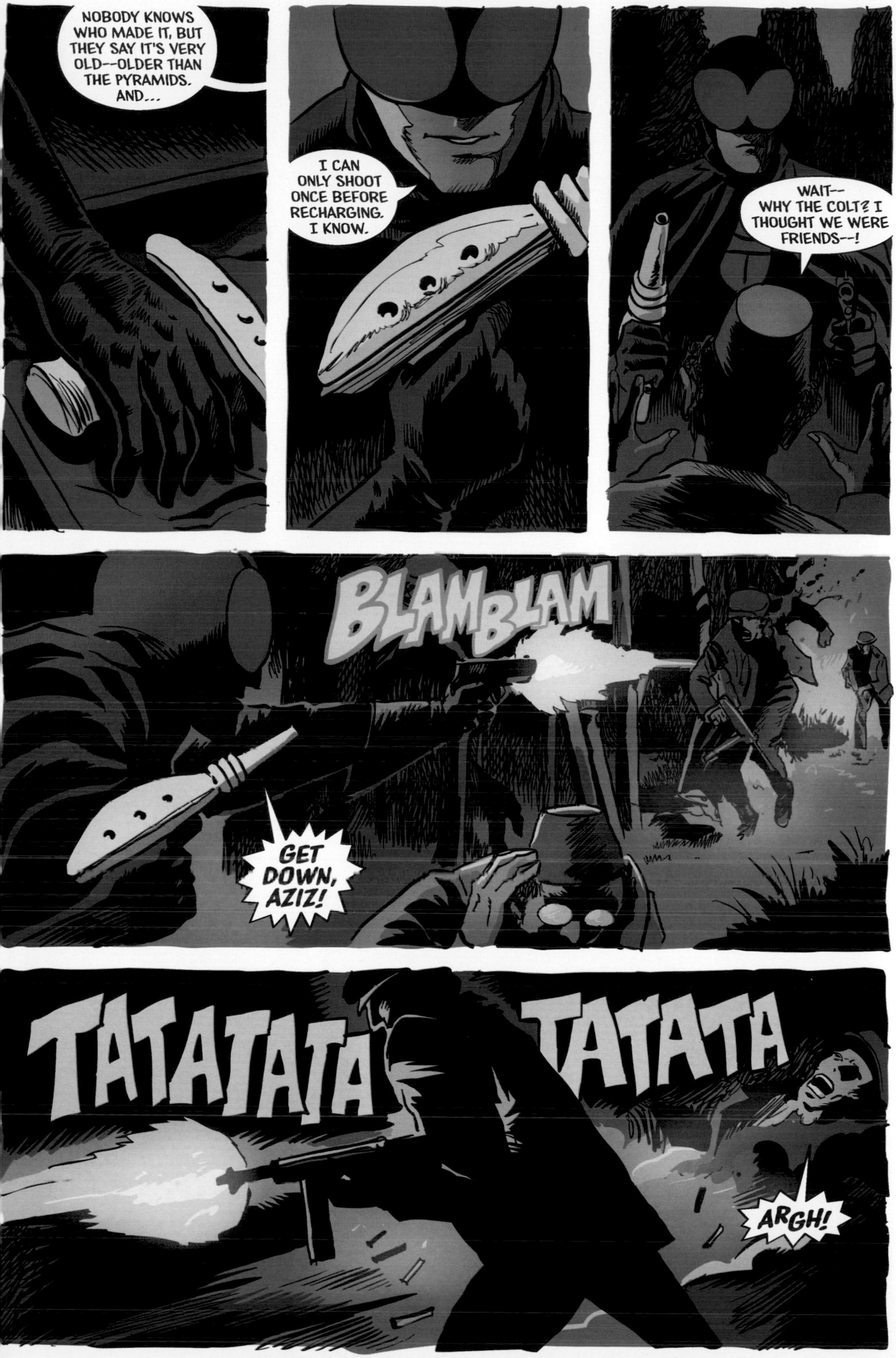
NOBODY KNOWS WHO MADE IT, BUT THEY SAY IT'S VERY OLD--OLDER THAN THE PYRAMIDS. AND...
I CAN ONLY SHOOT ONCE BEFORE RECHARGING. I KNOW.
WAIT-- WHY THE COLT? I THOUGHT WE WERE FRIENDS--!
BLAMBLAM
GET DOWN, AZIZ!
TATATATA
TATATA
ARGH!

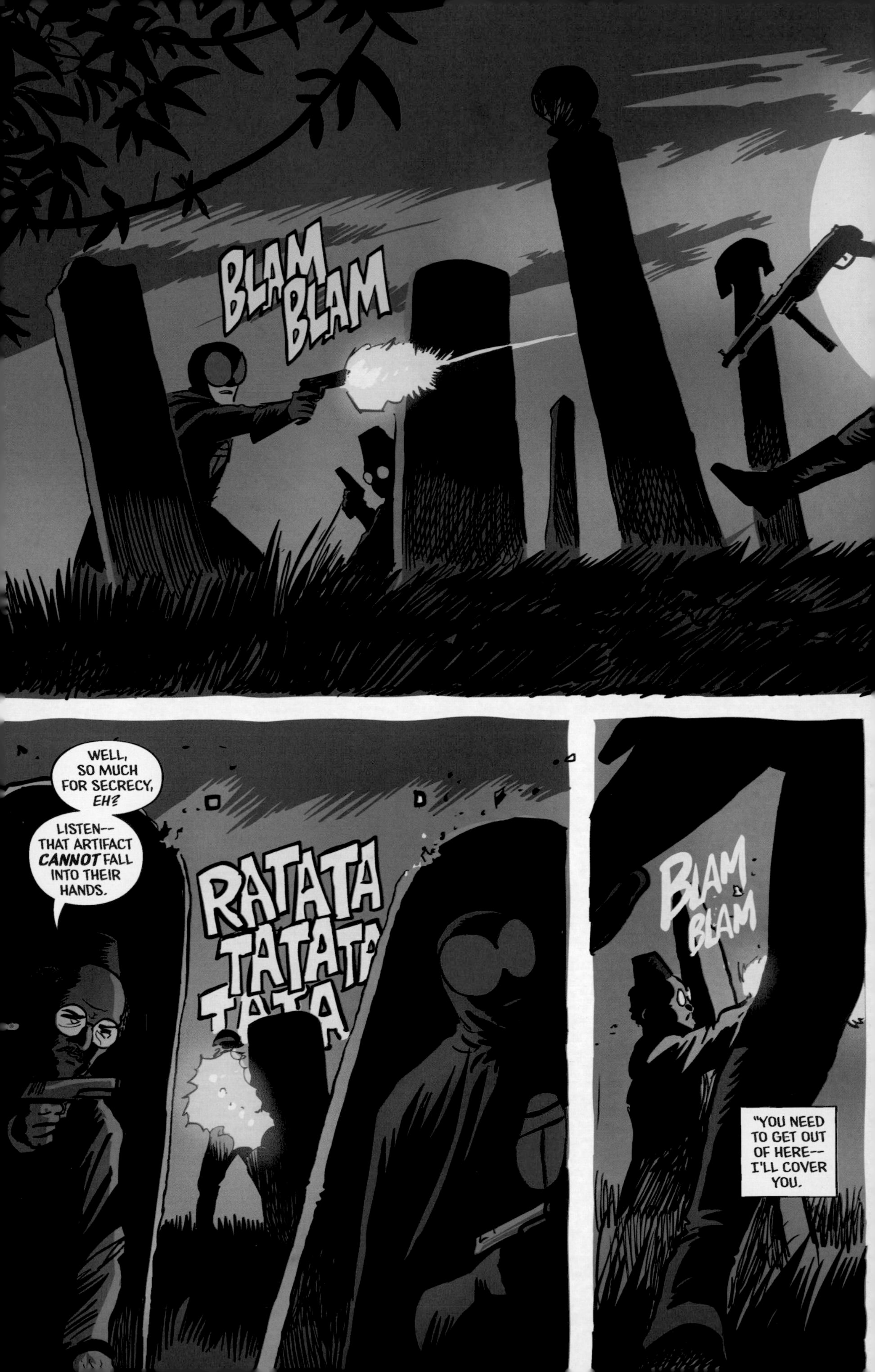

BLAM BLAM
WELL, SO MUCH FOR SECRECY, EH?
LISTEN-- THAT ARTIFACT CANNOT FALL INTO THEIR HANDS.
RATATA TATATA
BLAM BLAM
"YOU NEED TO GET OUT OF HERE-- I'LL COVER YOU.

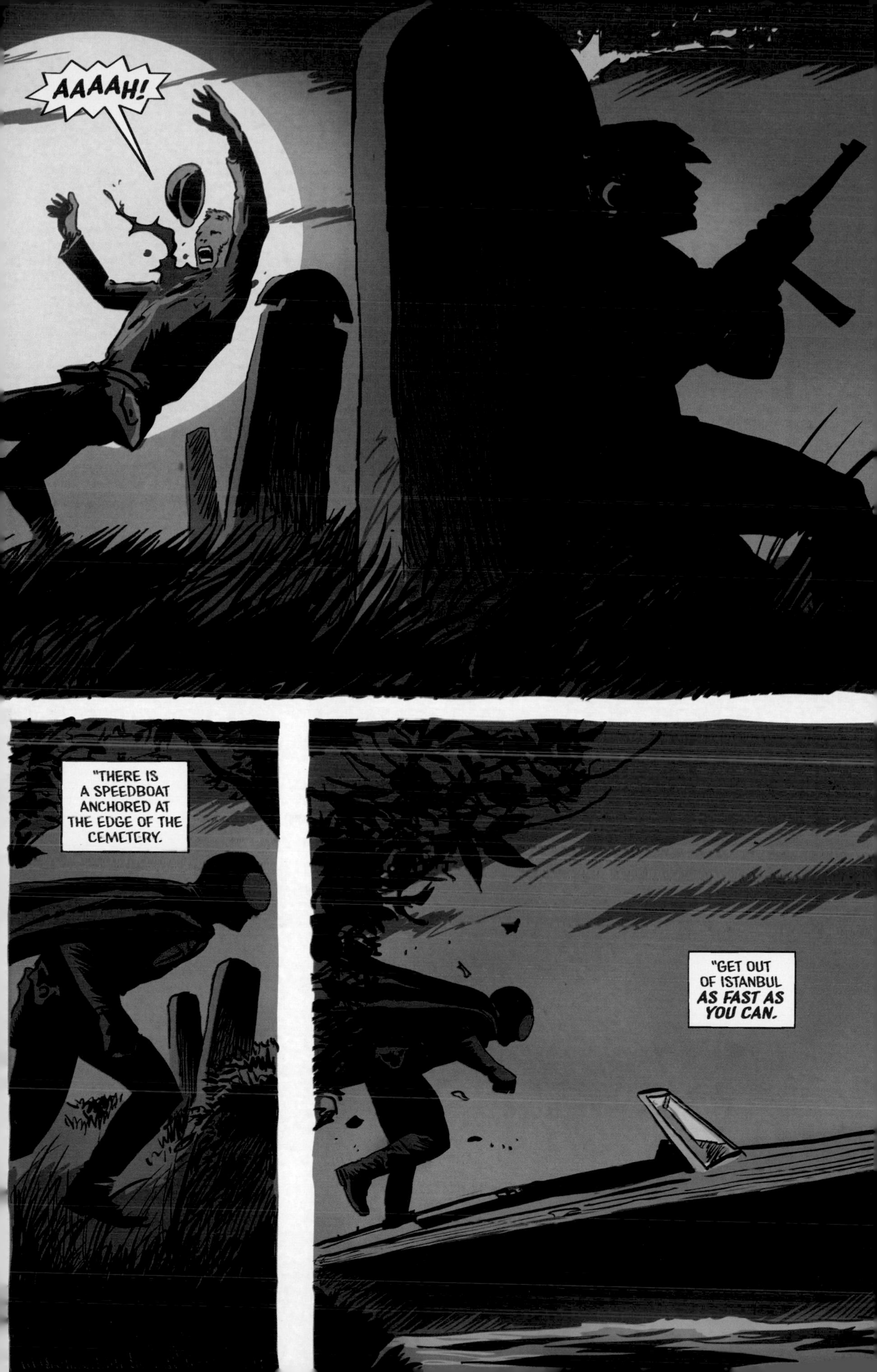
AAAAH!
"THERE IS A SPEEDBOAT ANCHORED AT THE EDGE OF THE CEMETERY.
"GET OUT OF ISTANBUL AS FAST AS YOU CAN.

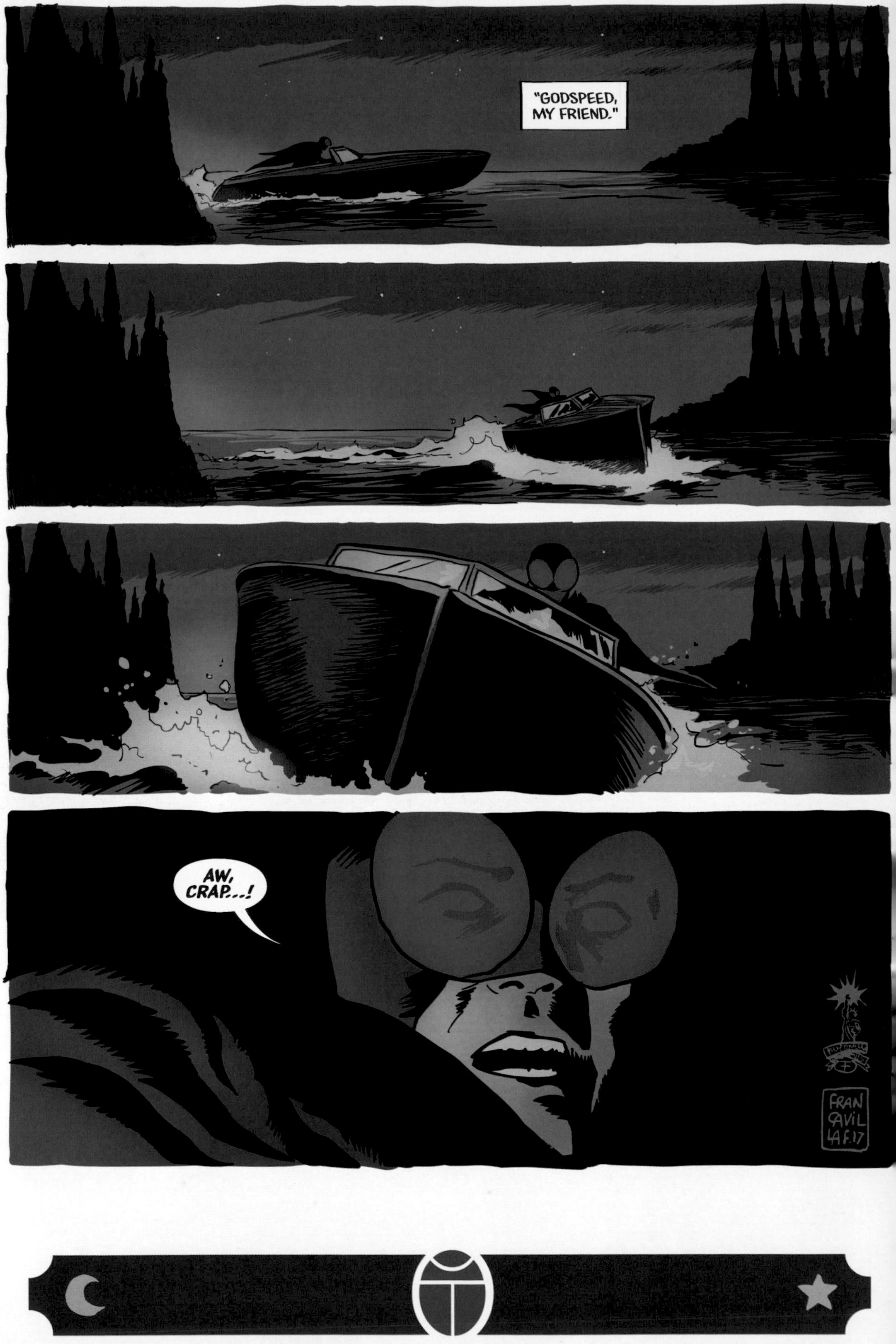
"GODSPEED, MY FRIEND."
AW, CRAP...!
FRAN CAVIL LA F.17

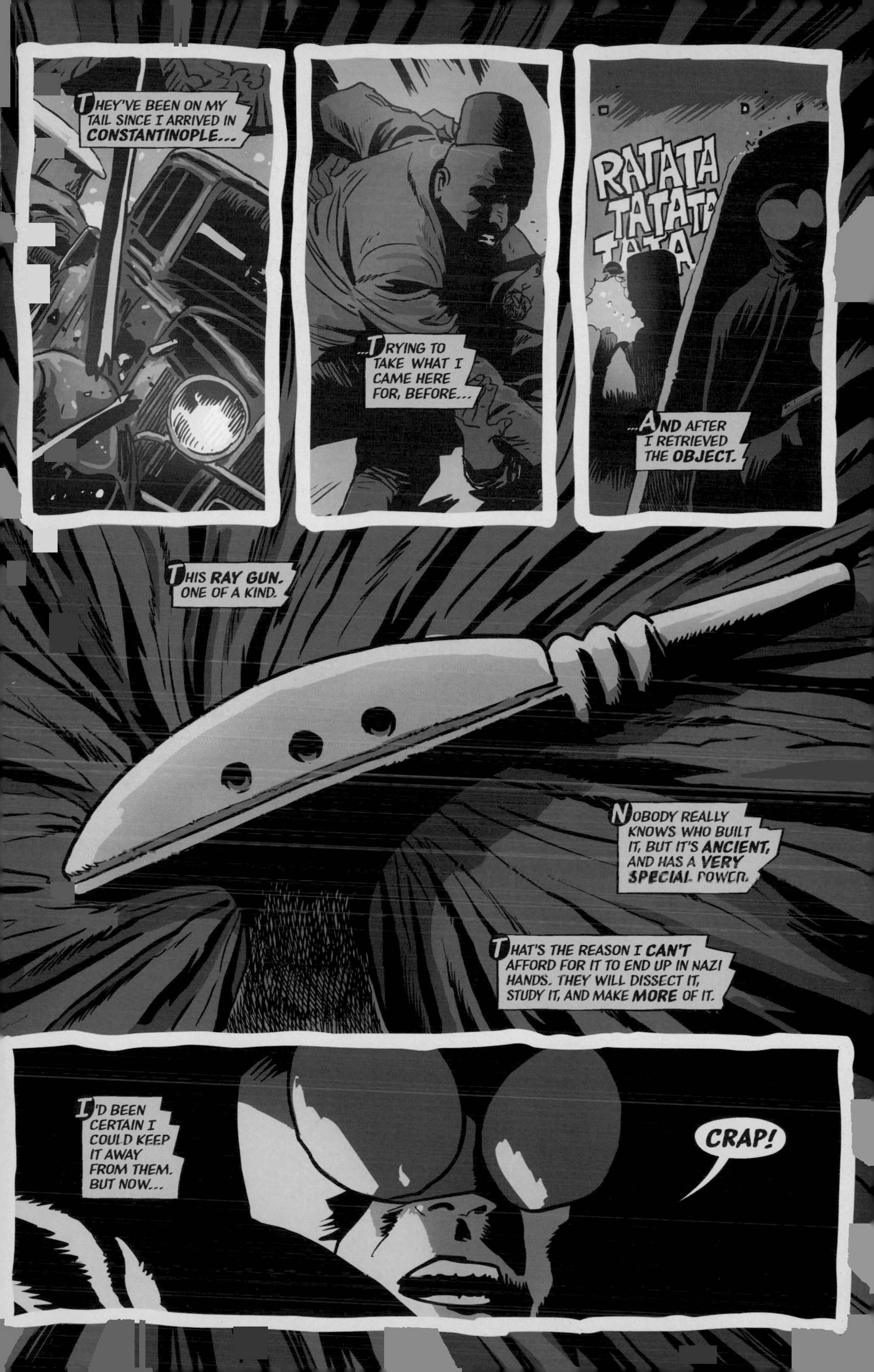
THEY'VE BEEN ON MY TAIL SINCE I ARRIVED IN CONSTANTINOPLE...
...TRYING TO TAKE WHAT I CAME HERE FOR, BEFORE...
RATATA TATATA TATA
...AND AFTER I RETRIEVED THE OBJECT.
THIS RAY GUN. ONE OF A KIND.
NOBODY REALLY KNOWS WHO BUILT IT, BUT IT'S ANCIENT, AND HAS A VERY SPECIAL POWER.
THAT'S THE REASON I CAN'T AFFORD FOR IT TO END UP IN NAZI HANDS. THEY WILL DISSECT IT, STUDY IT, AND MAKE MORE OF IT.
I'D BEEN CERTAIN I COULD KEEP IT AWAY FROM THEM. BUT NOW...
CRAP!

Chapter Five

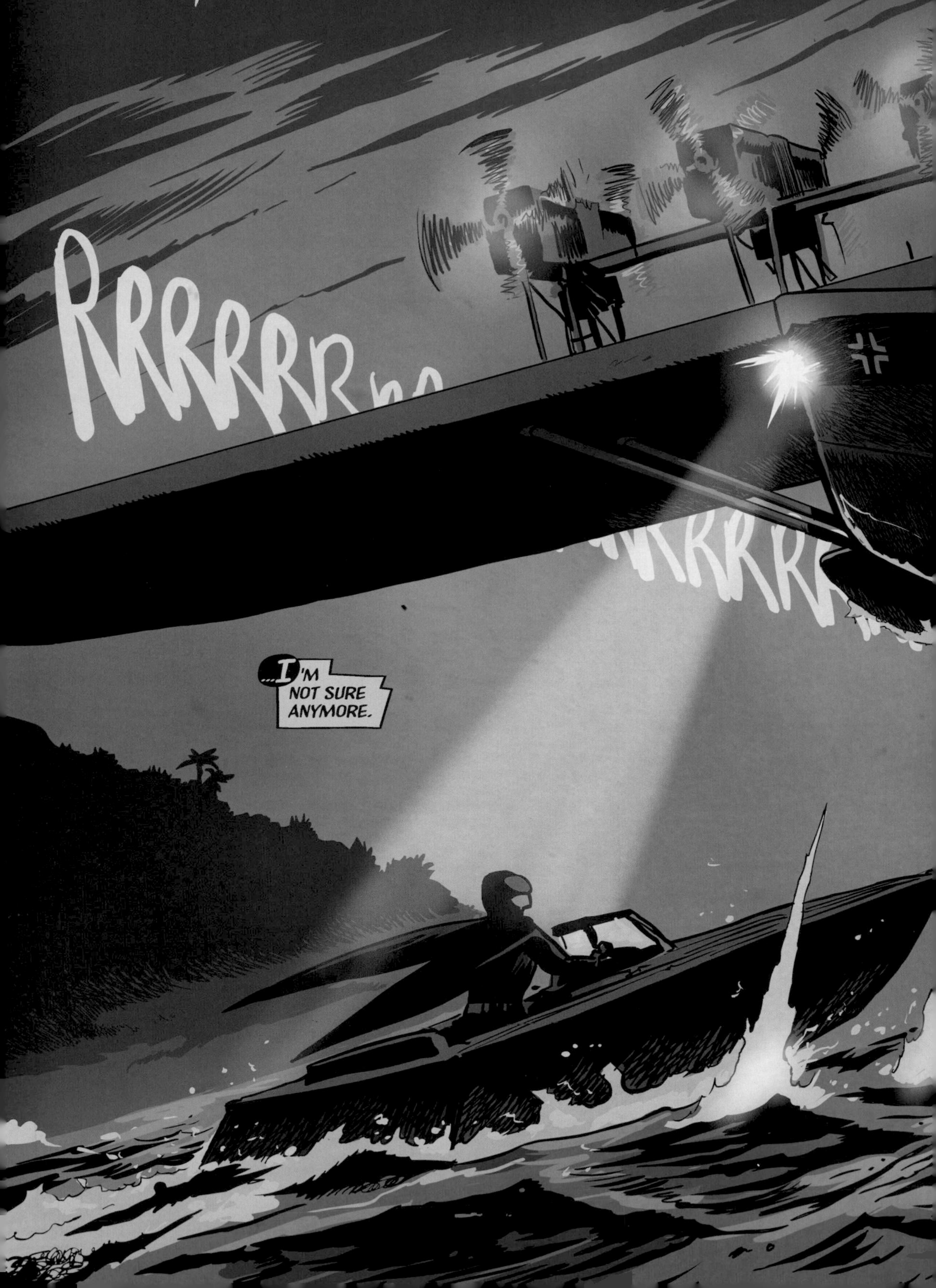
RRRRRRRR
RRRRR
...I'M NOT SURE ANYMORE.

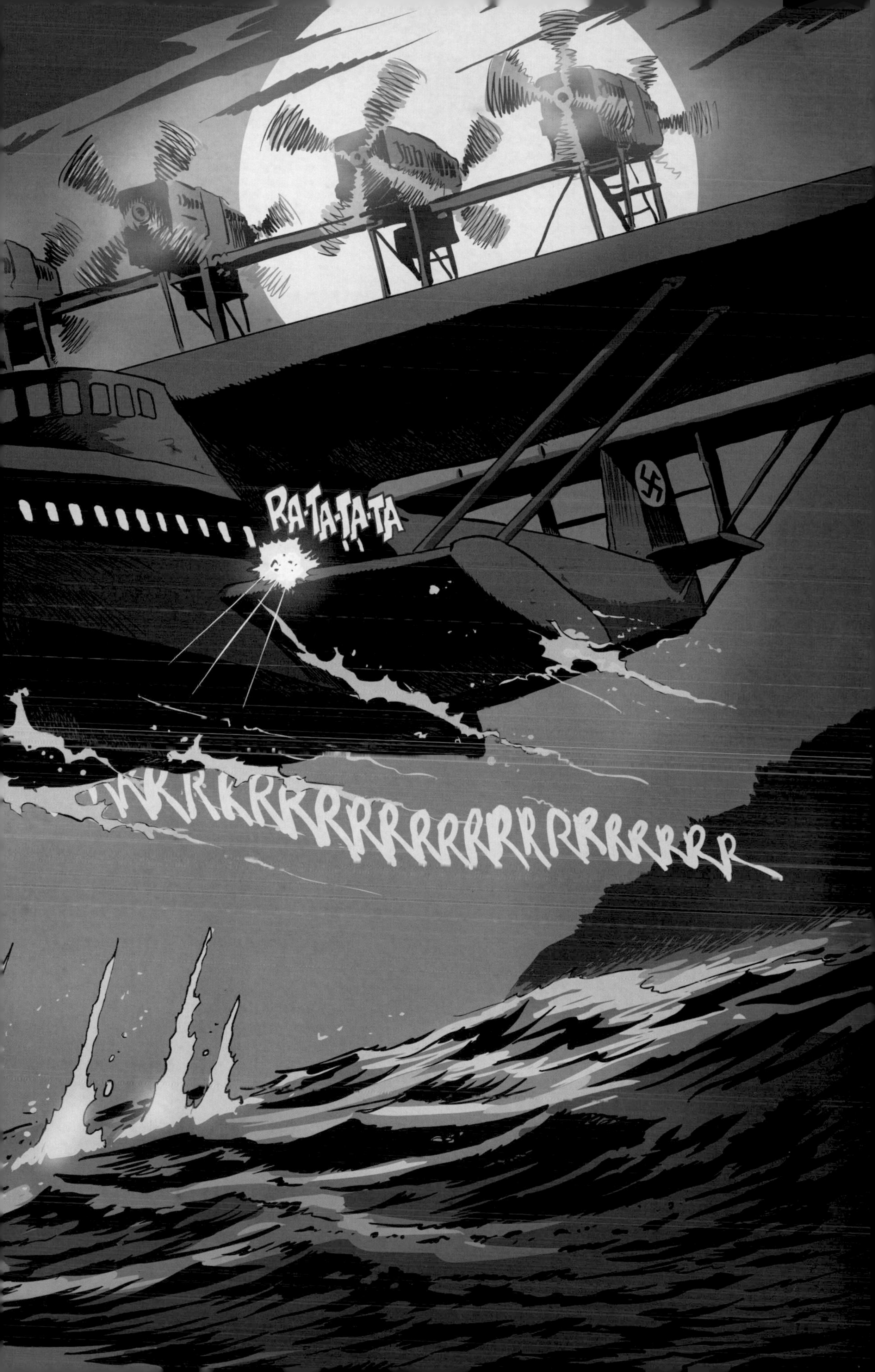
RA-TA-TA-TA
WRRRRRRRRRRRRRRRRRRRR

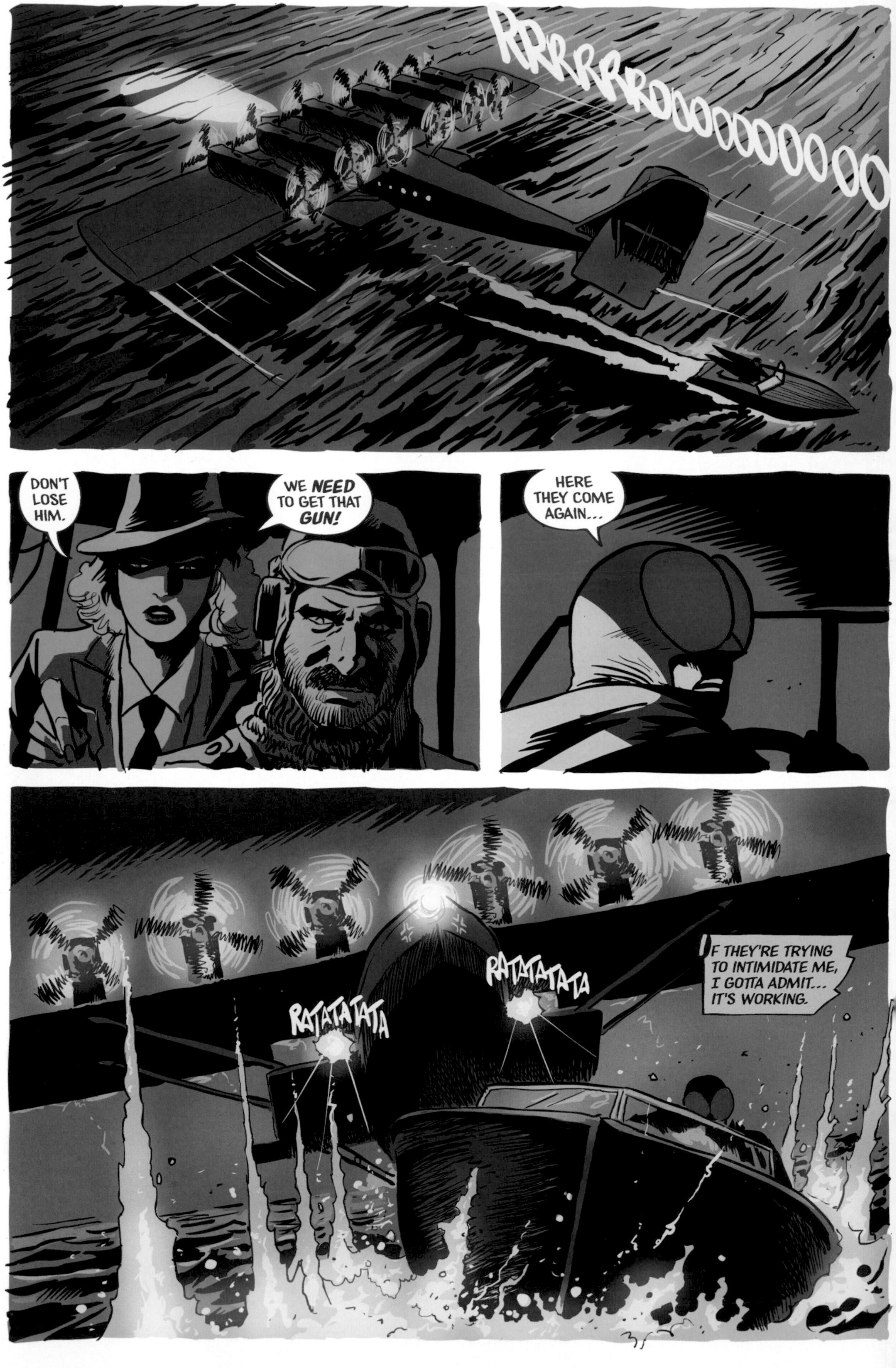
RRRRRRROOOOOOOOOOO
DON'T LOSE HIM.
WE NEED TO GET THAT GUN!
HERE THEY COME AGAIN...
IF THEY'RE TRYING TO INTIMIDATE ME, I GOTTA ADMIT... IT'S WORKING.
RATATATATA
RATATATATA

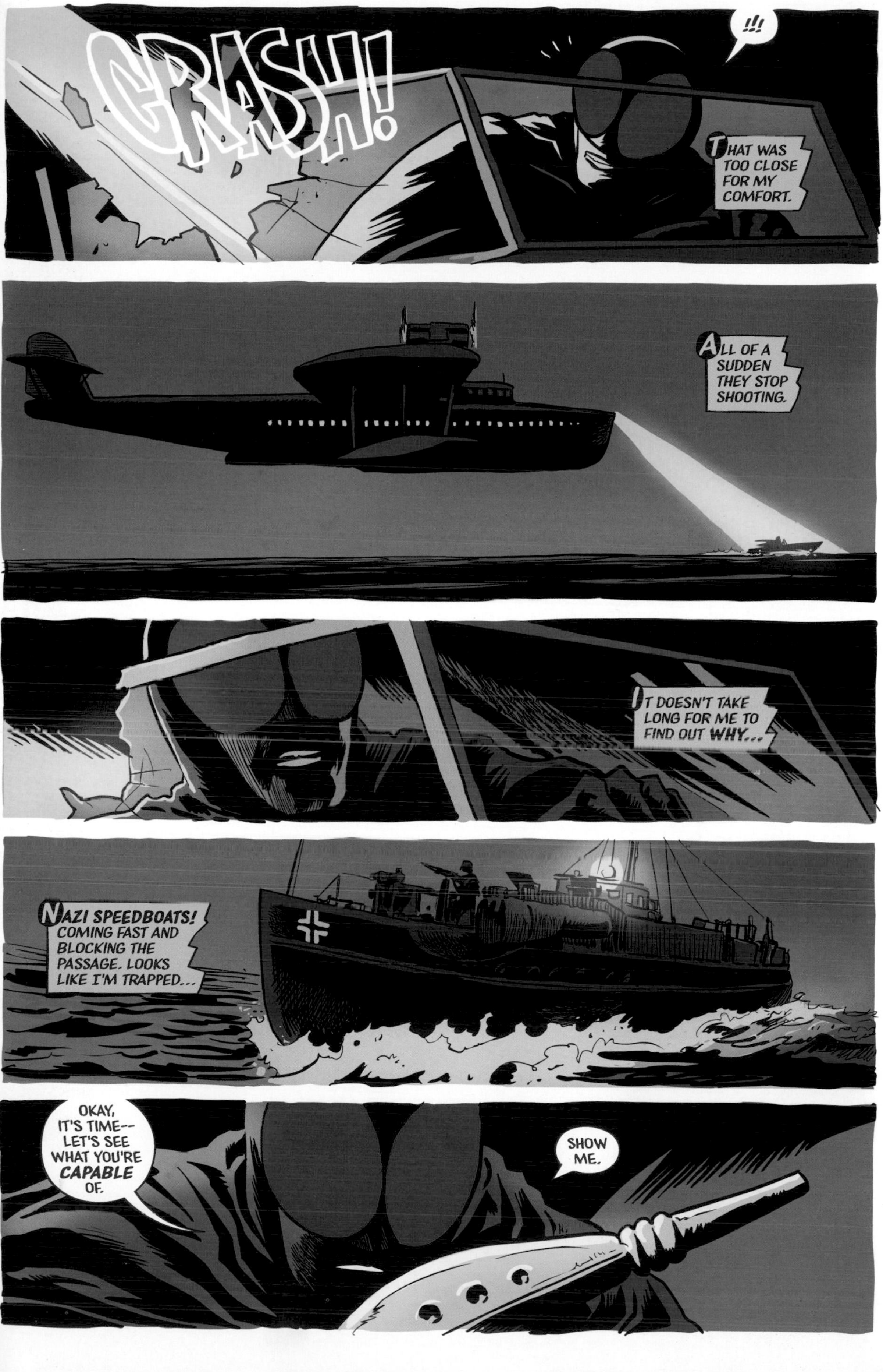
CRASH!
!!!
THAT WAS TOO CLOSE FOR MY COMFORT.
ALL OF A SUDDEN THEY STOP SHOOTING.
IT DOESN'T TAKE LONG FOR ME TO FIND OUT WHY...
NAZI SPEEDBOATS! COMING FAST AND BLOCKING THE PASSAGE. LOOKS LIKE I'M TRAPPED...
OKAY, IT'S TIME-- LET'S SEE WHAT YOU'RE CAPABLE OF.
SHOW ME.

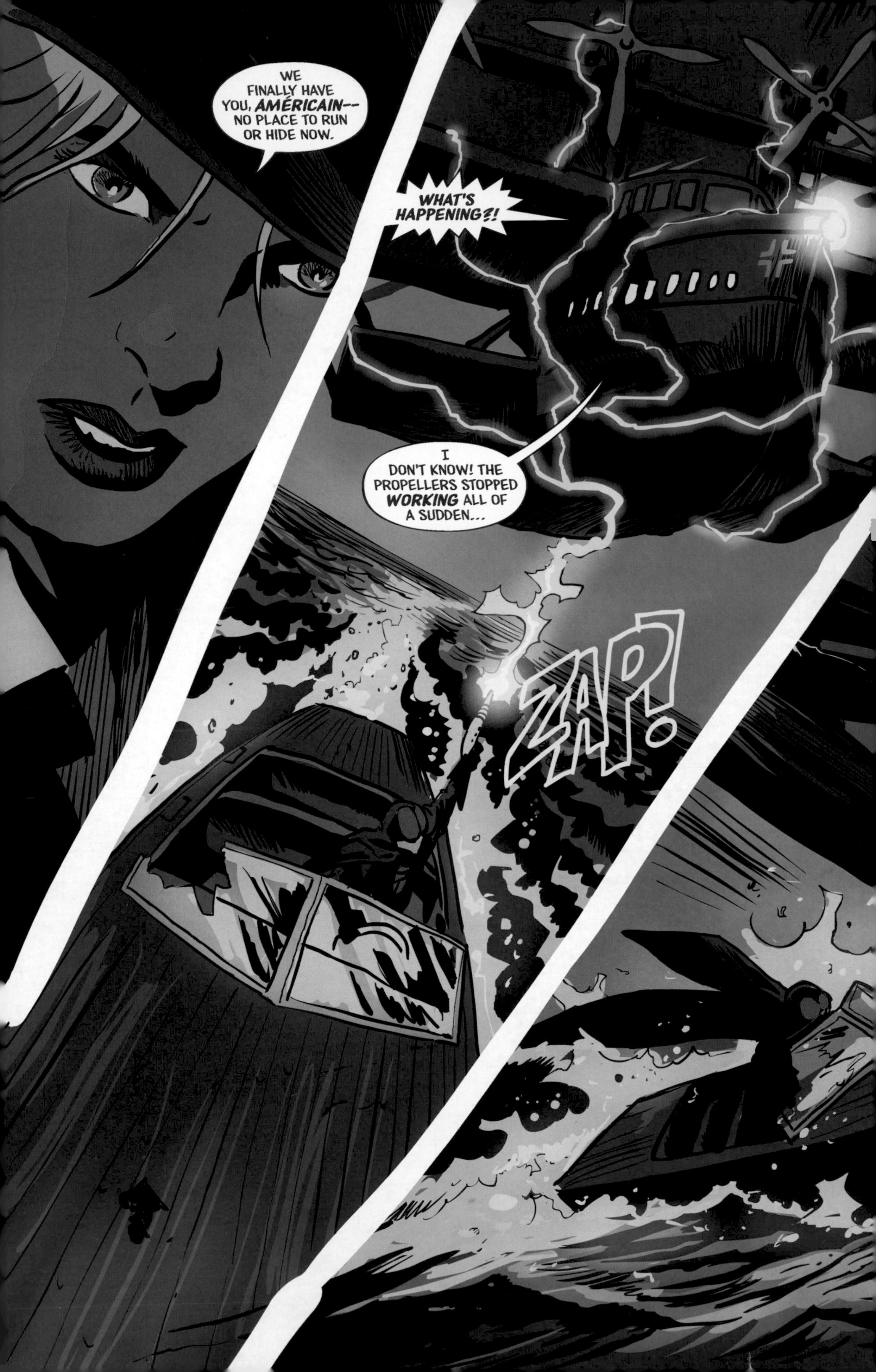
WE FINALLY HAVE YOU, AMÉRICAIN-- NO PLACE TO RUN OR HIDE NOW.
WHAT'S HAPPENING?!
I DON'T KNOW! THE PROPELLERS STOPPED WORKING ALL OF A SUDDEN...
ZAP!

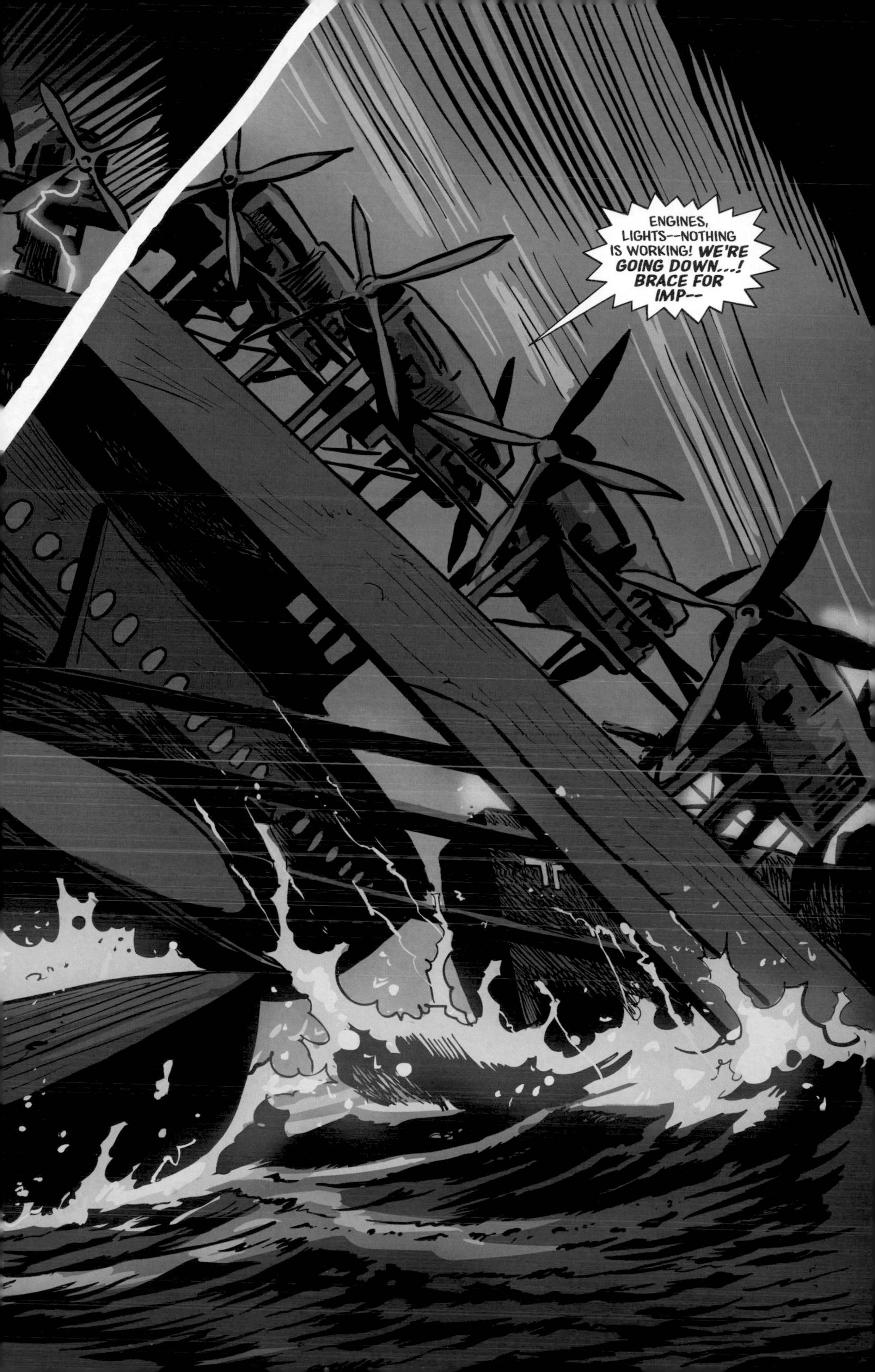
ENGINES, LIGHTS--NOTHING IS WORKING! WE'RE GOING DOWN...! BRACE FOR IMP--

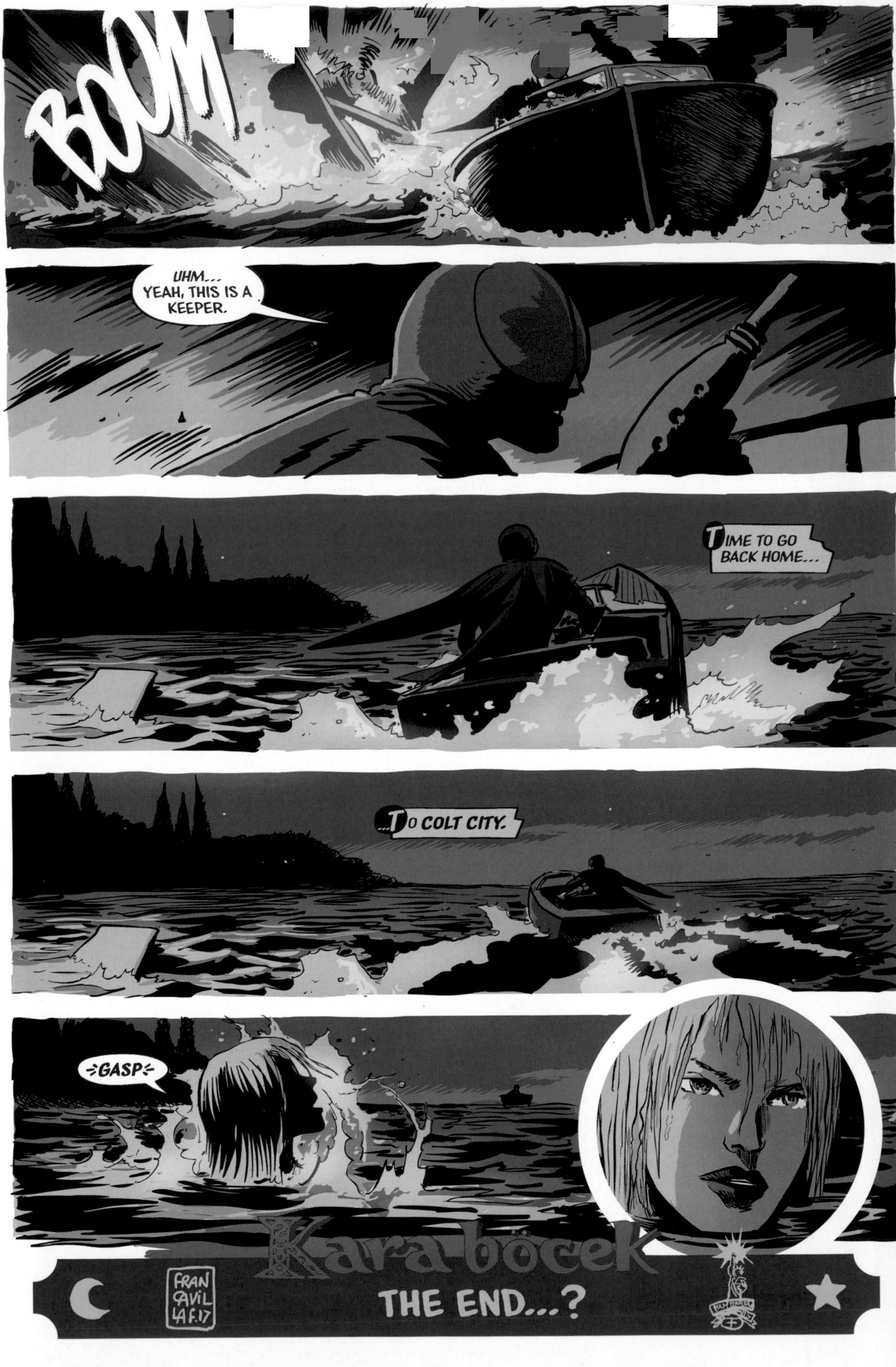
BOOM
UHM... YEAH, THIS IS A KEEPER.
TIME TO GO BACK HOME...
...TO COLT CITY.
GASP
Kara böcek
FRAN CAVIL LA F.17
THE END...?

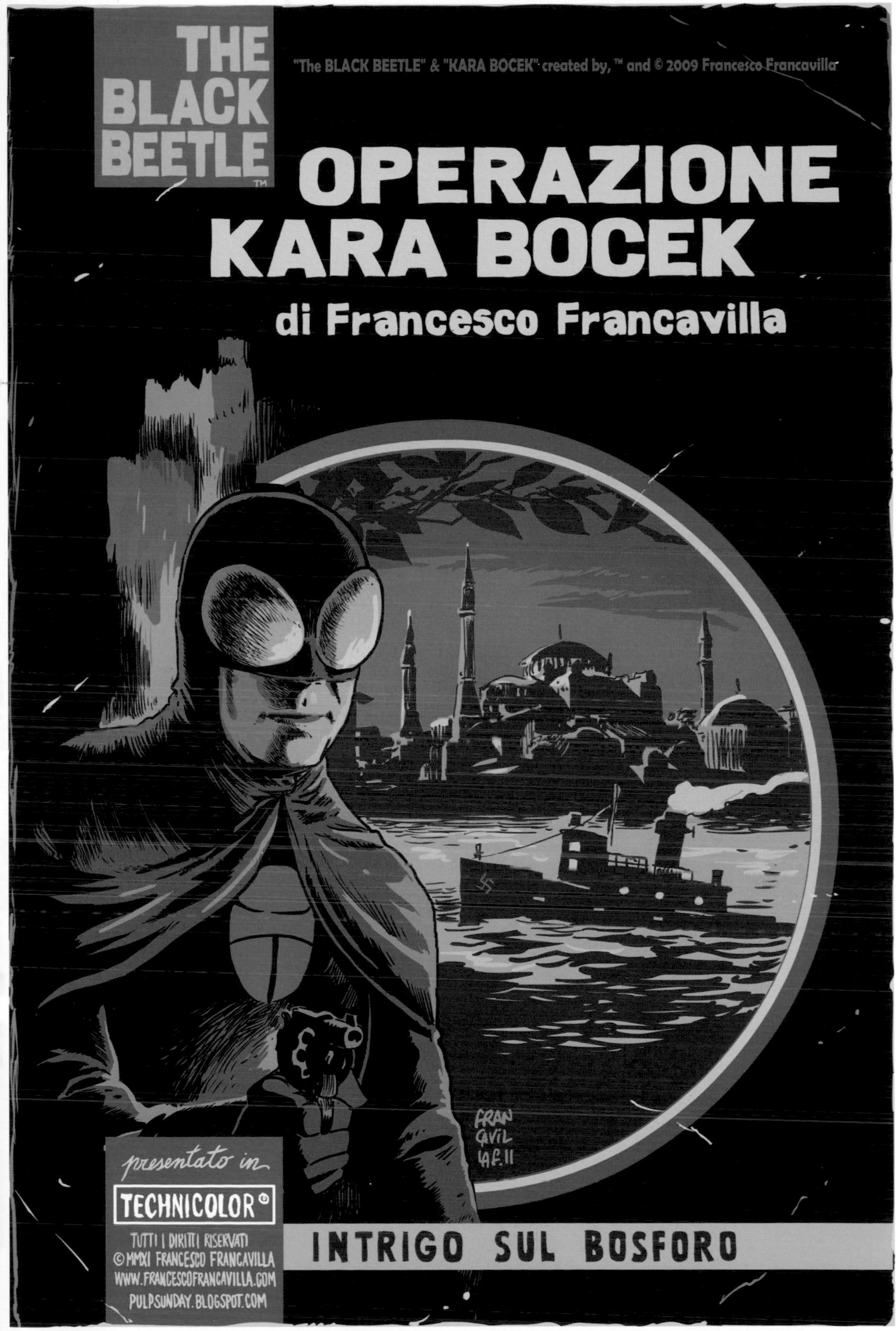
THE BLACK BEETLE™
"The BLACK BEETLE" & "KARA BOCEK" created by, ™ and © 2009 Francesco Francavilla
OPERAZIONE KARA BOCEK
di Francesco Francavilla
FRAN CAVIL LA.f.11
presentato in
TECHNICOLOR
TUTTI I DIRITTI RISERVATI
© MMXI FRANCESCO FRANCAVILLA
WWW.FRANCESCOFRANCAVILLA.COM
PULPSUNDAY.BLOGSPOT.COM
INTRIGO SUL BOSFORO

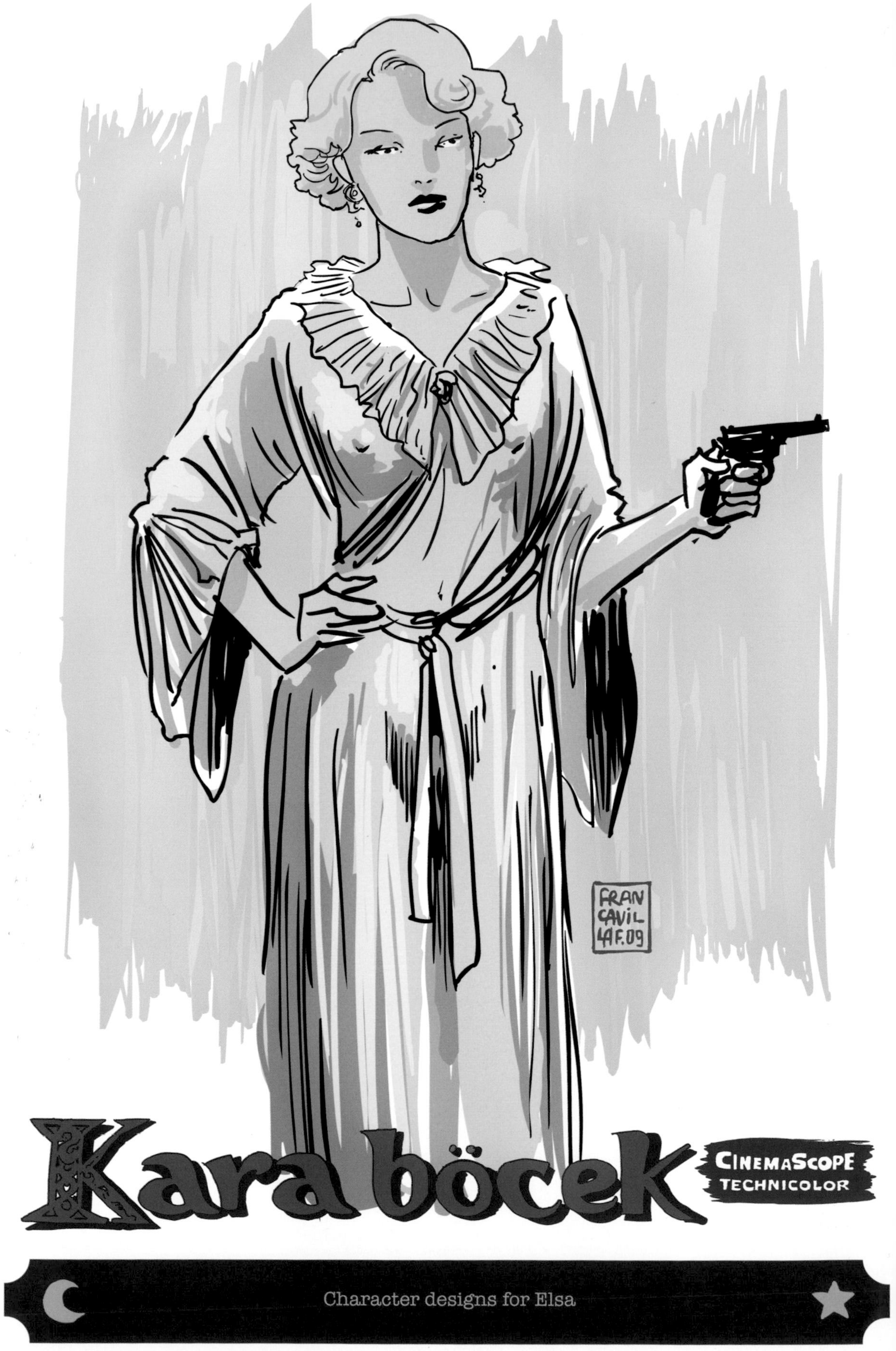
FRAN
CAVIL
LA F.09
Karaböcek
CINEMASCOPE
TECHNICOLOR

Character designs for Elsa

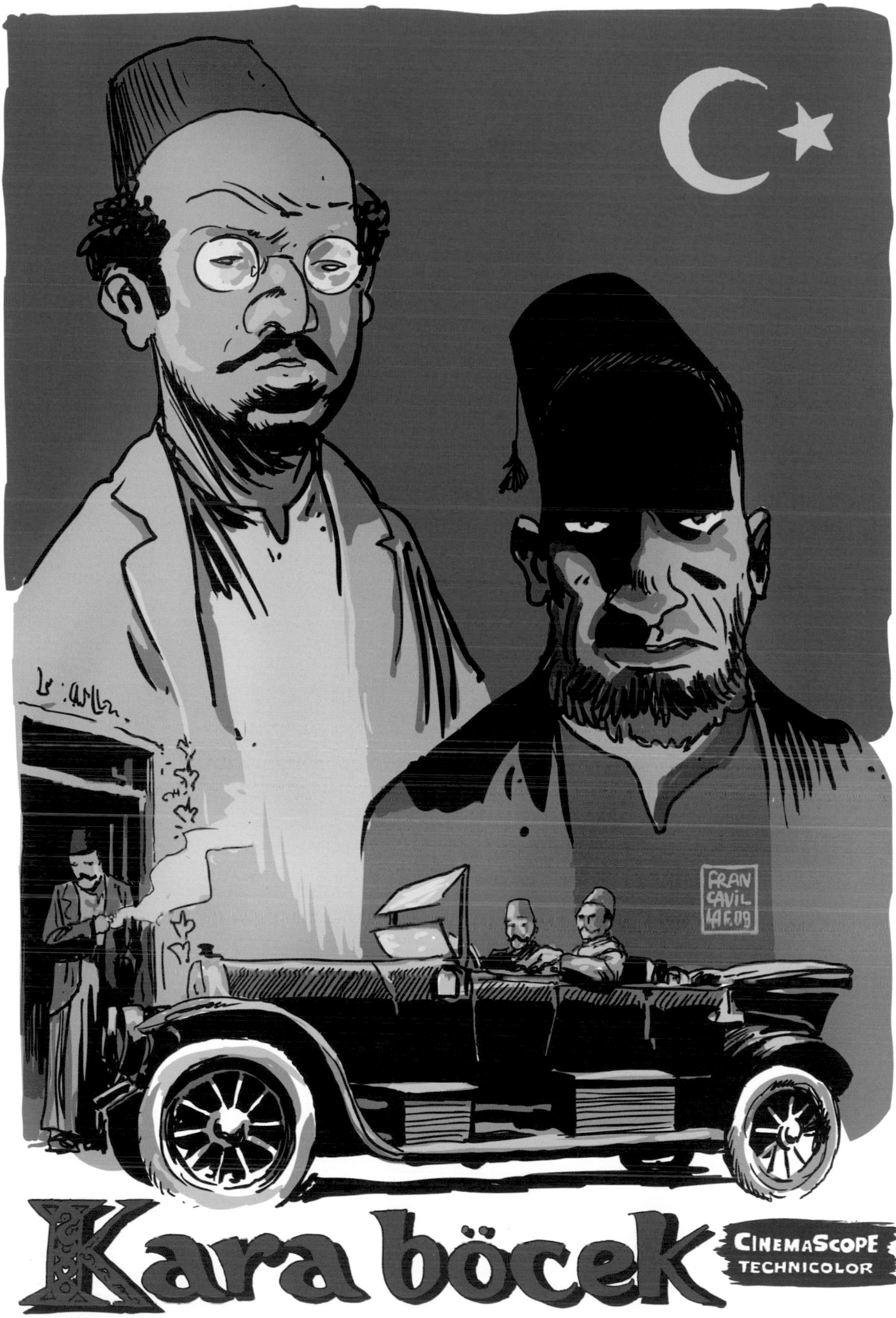
FRAN
CAVIL
LA F.09
Kara böcek
CinemaScope
TECHNICOLOR

Character designs for Aziz and Ihsan

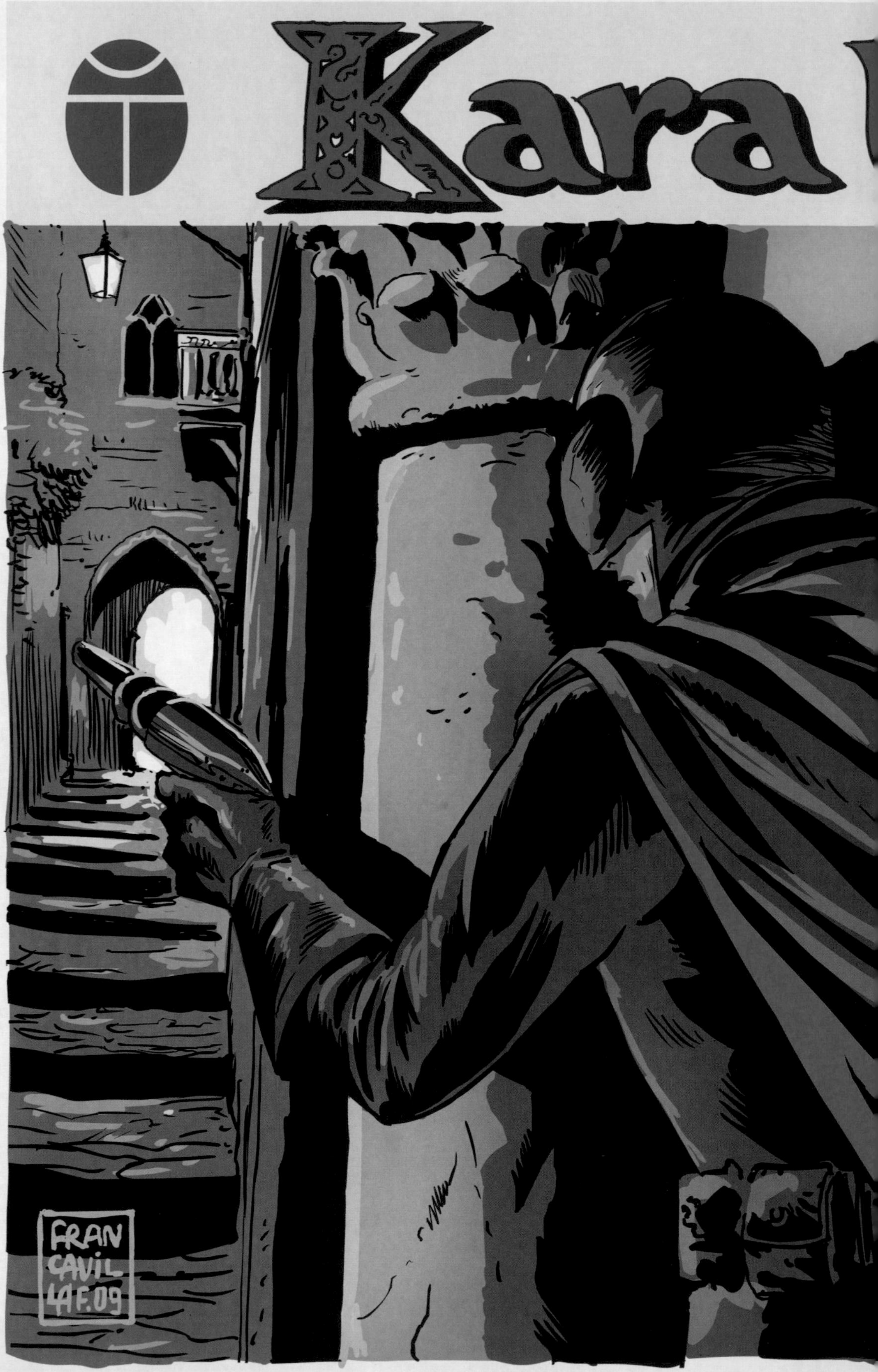

Kara
FRAN
CAVIL
LA F.09

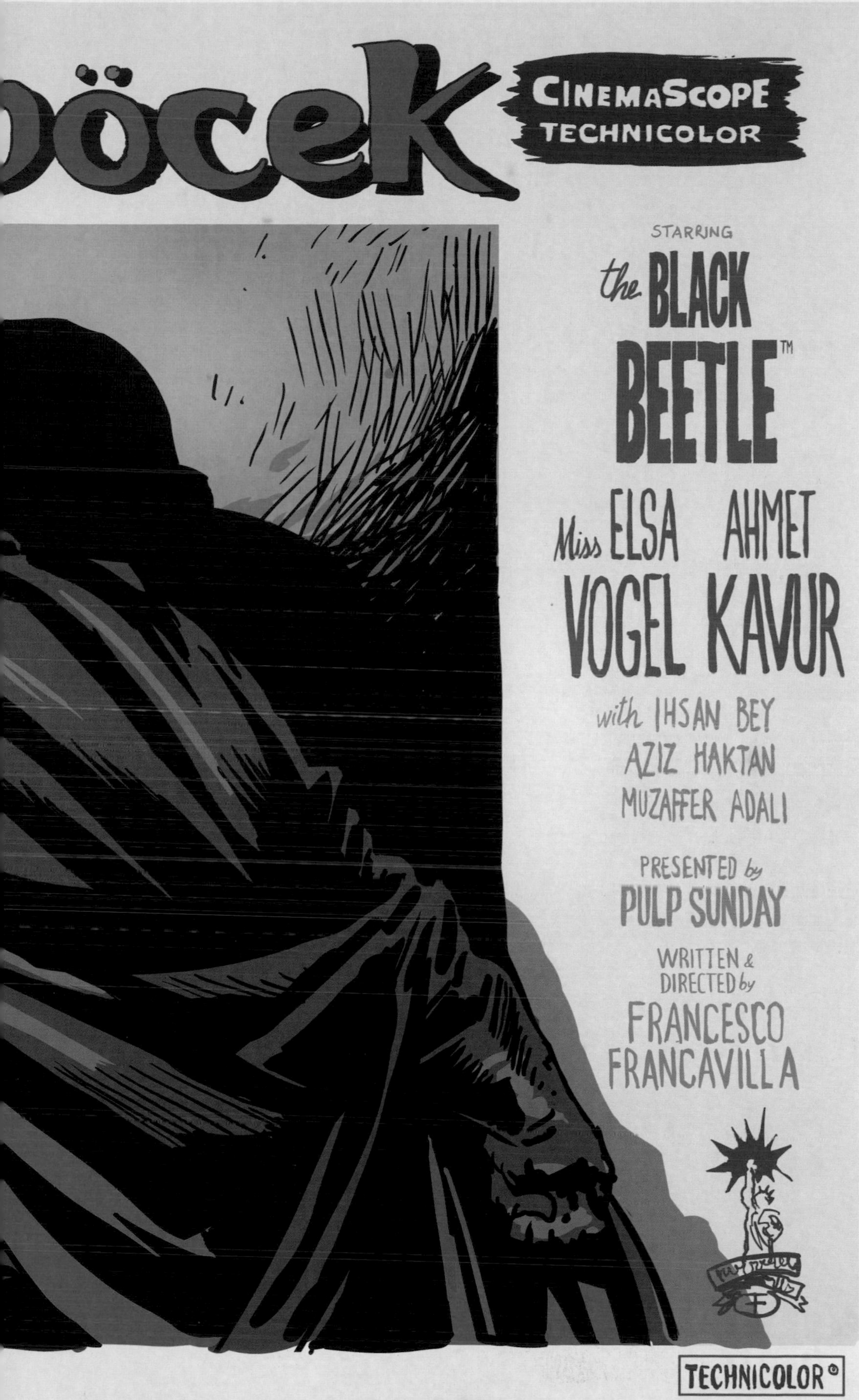

öcek
CINEMASCOPE
TECHNICOLOR
STARRING
the BLACK BEETLE™
Miss ELSA VOGEL
AHMET KAVUR
with IHSAN BEY
AZIZ HAKTAN
MUZAFFER ADALI
PRESENTED by
PULP SUNDAY
WRITTEN & DIRECTED by
FRANCESCO FRANCAVILLA
TECHNICOLOR©

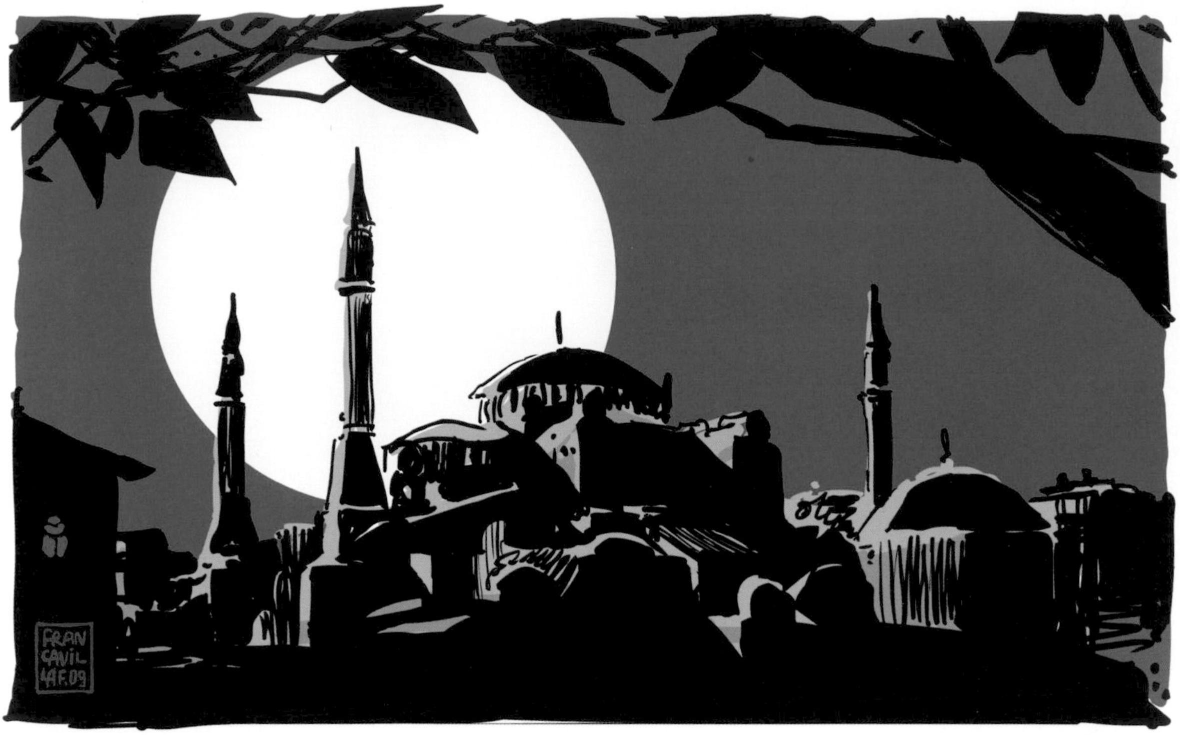
FRAN
GAVIL
14F.09

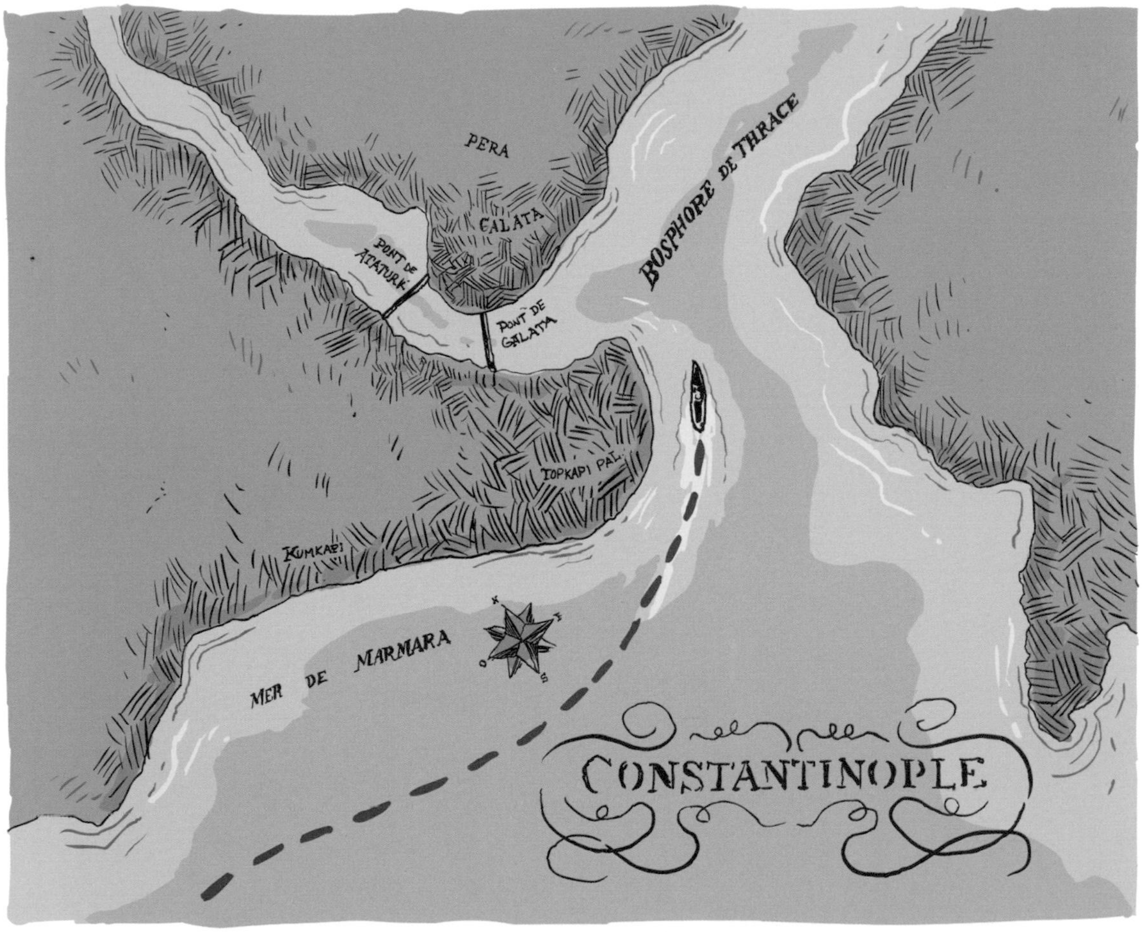
PERA
GALATA
PONT DE ATATURK
PONT DE GALATA
BOSPHORE DE THRACE
TOPKAPI PAL.
KUMKAPI
MER DE MARMARA
CONSTANTINOPLE

Location studies

Kara böcek

LAYOUTS

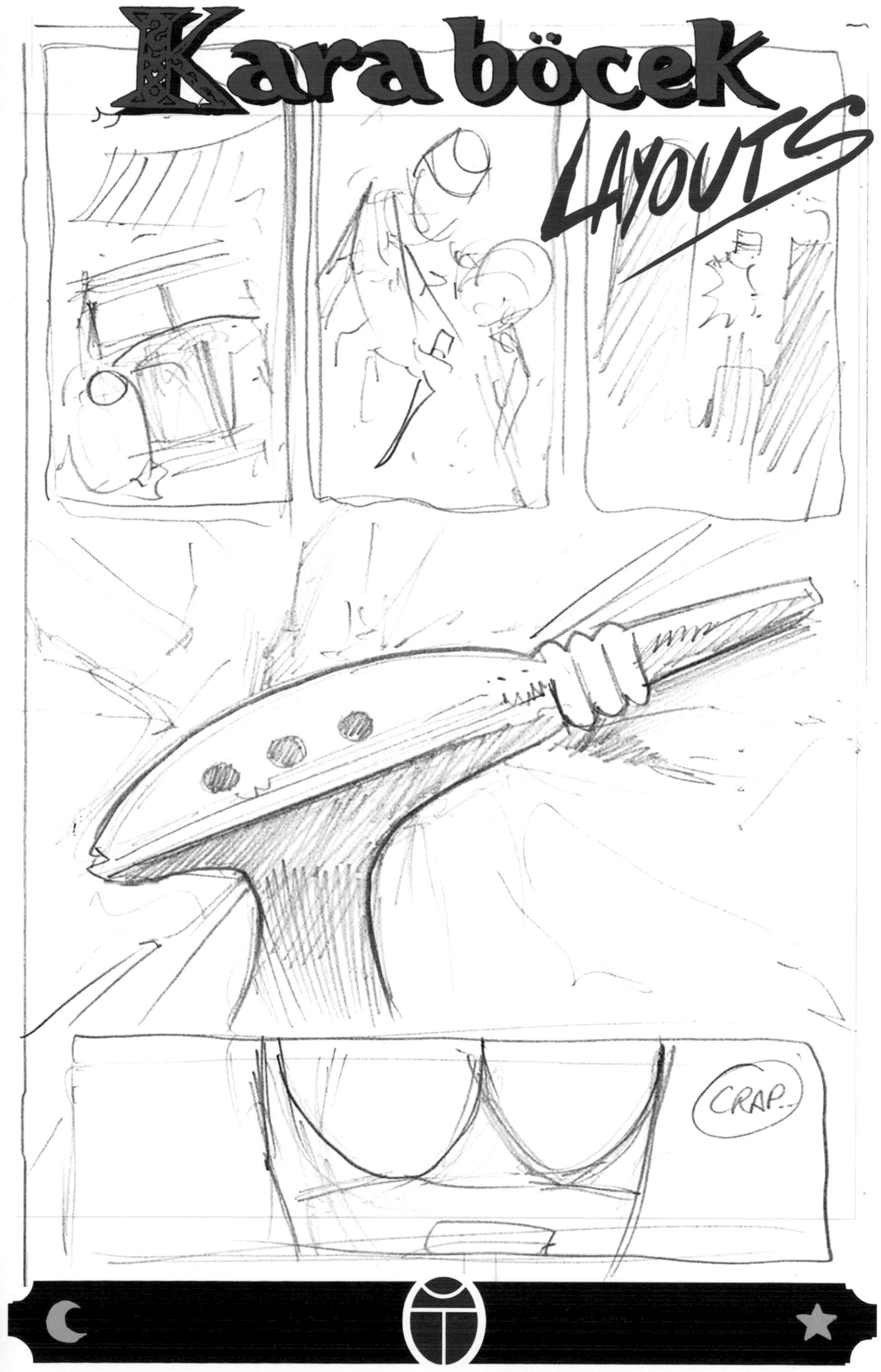
CRAP...

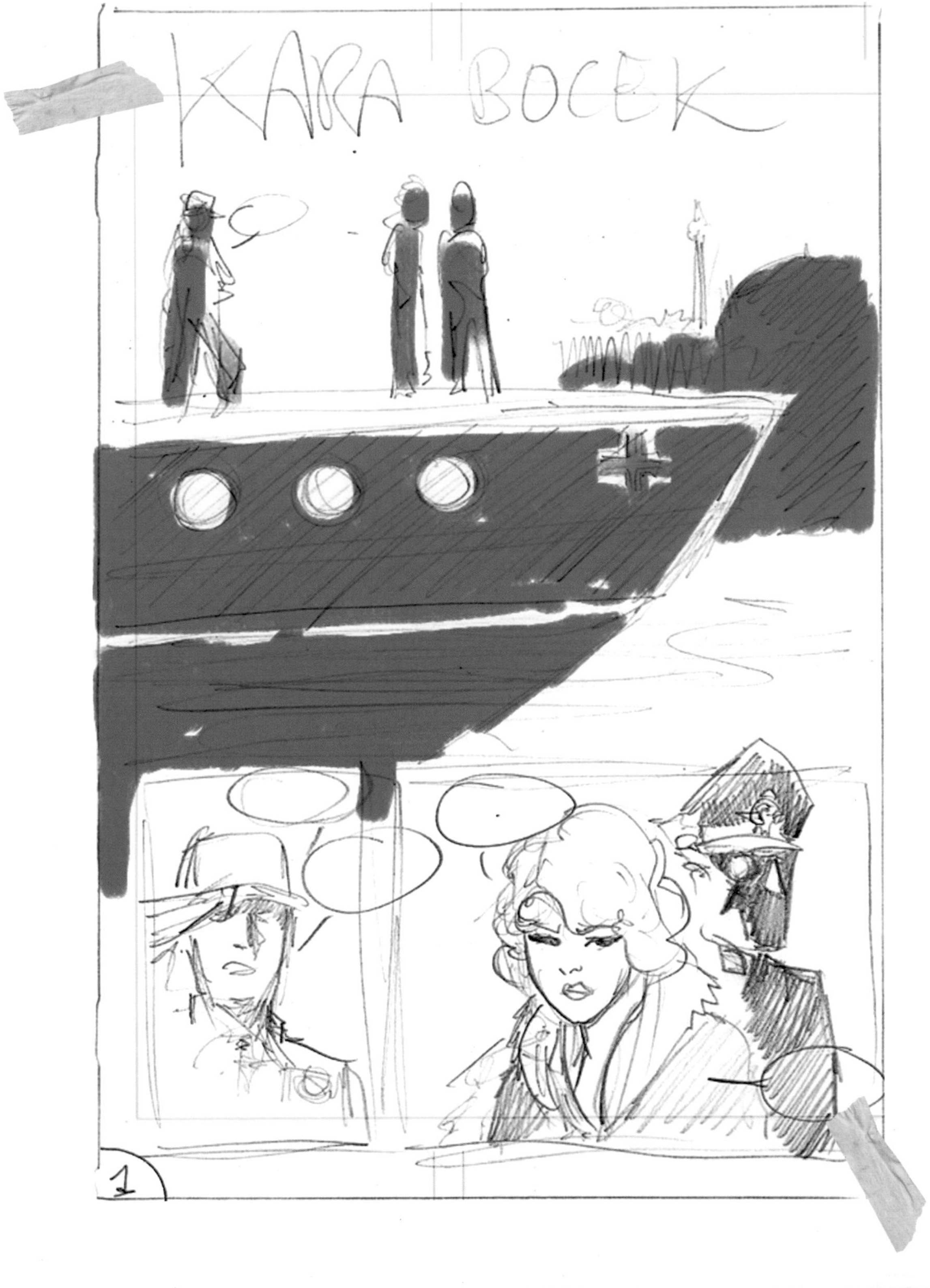
KARA BOCEK
1

Kara Böcek layouts

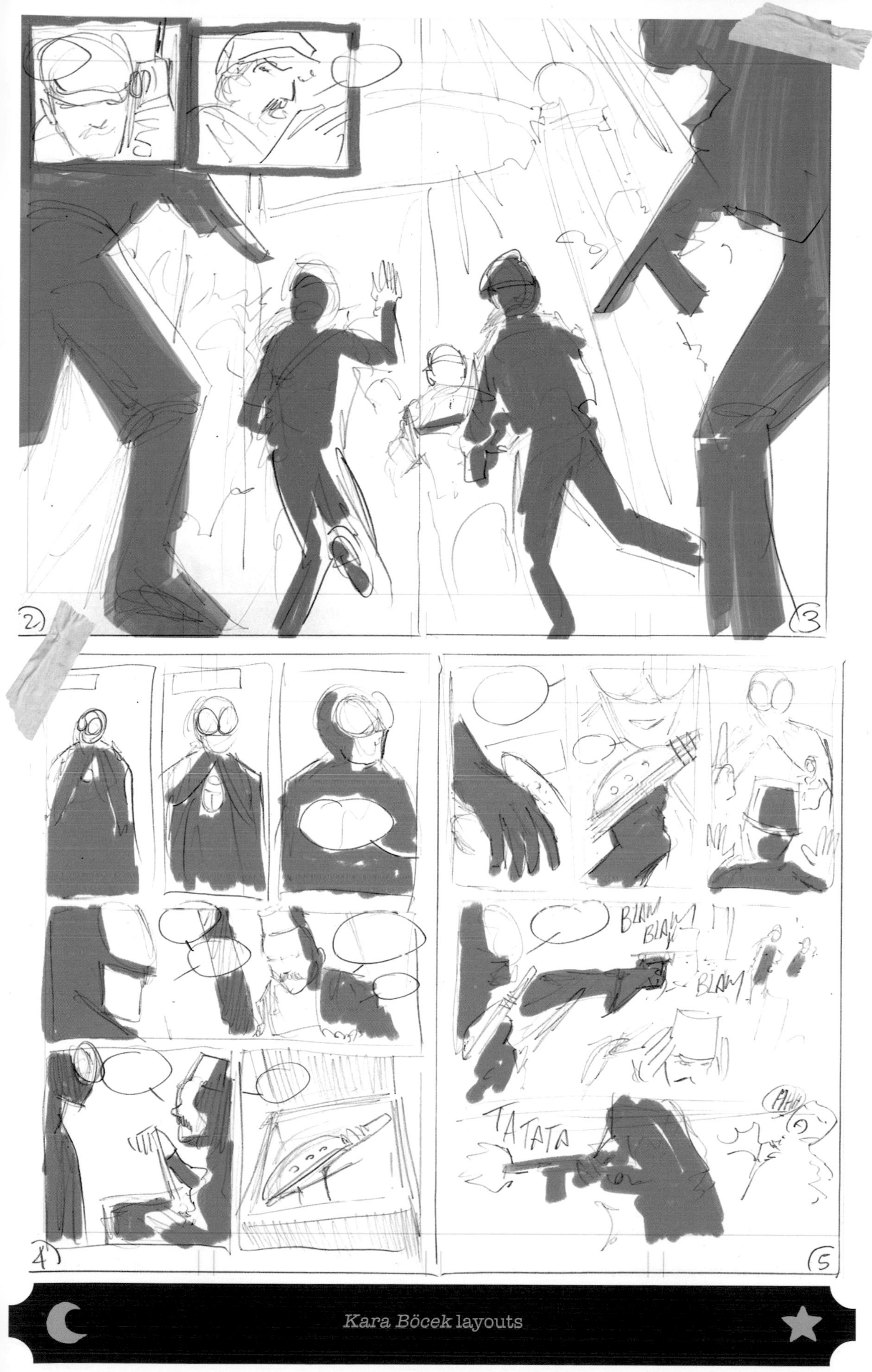
BLAM
BLAM
BLAM
TATATA

Kara Böcek layouts

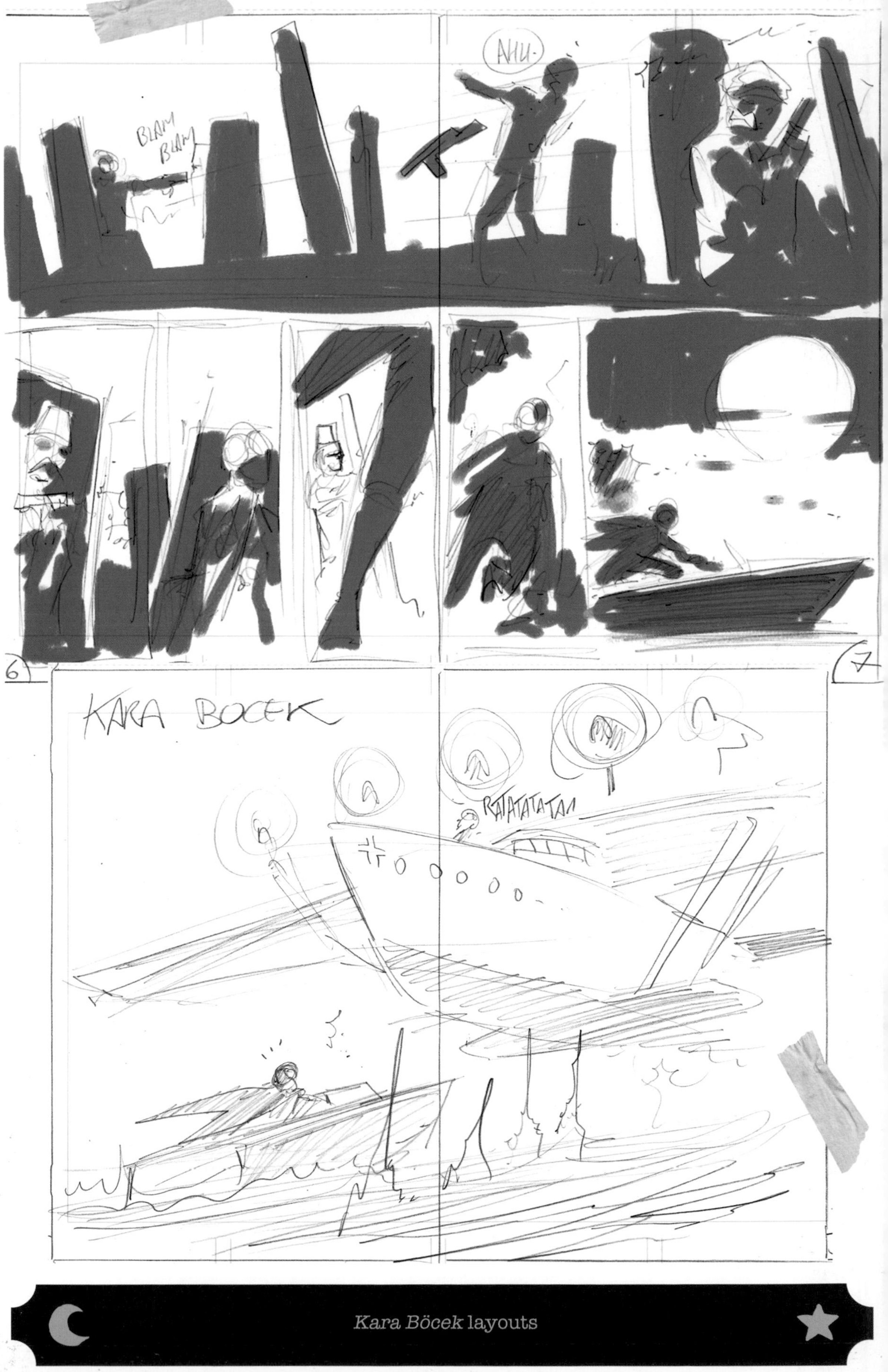

BLAM BLAM
AHU-
6
7
KARA BOCEK
RATATATATA

Kara Böcek layouts

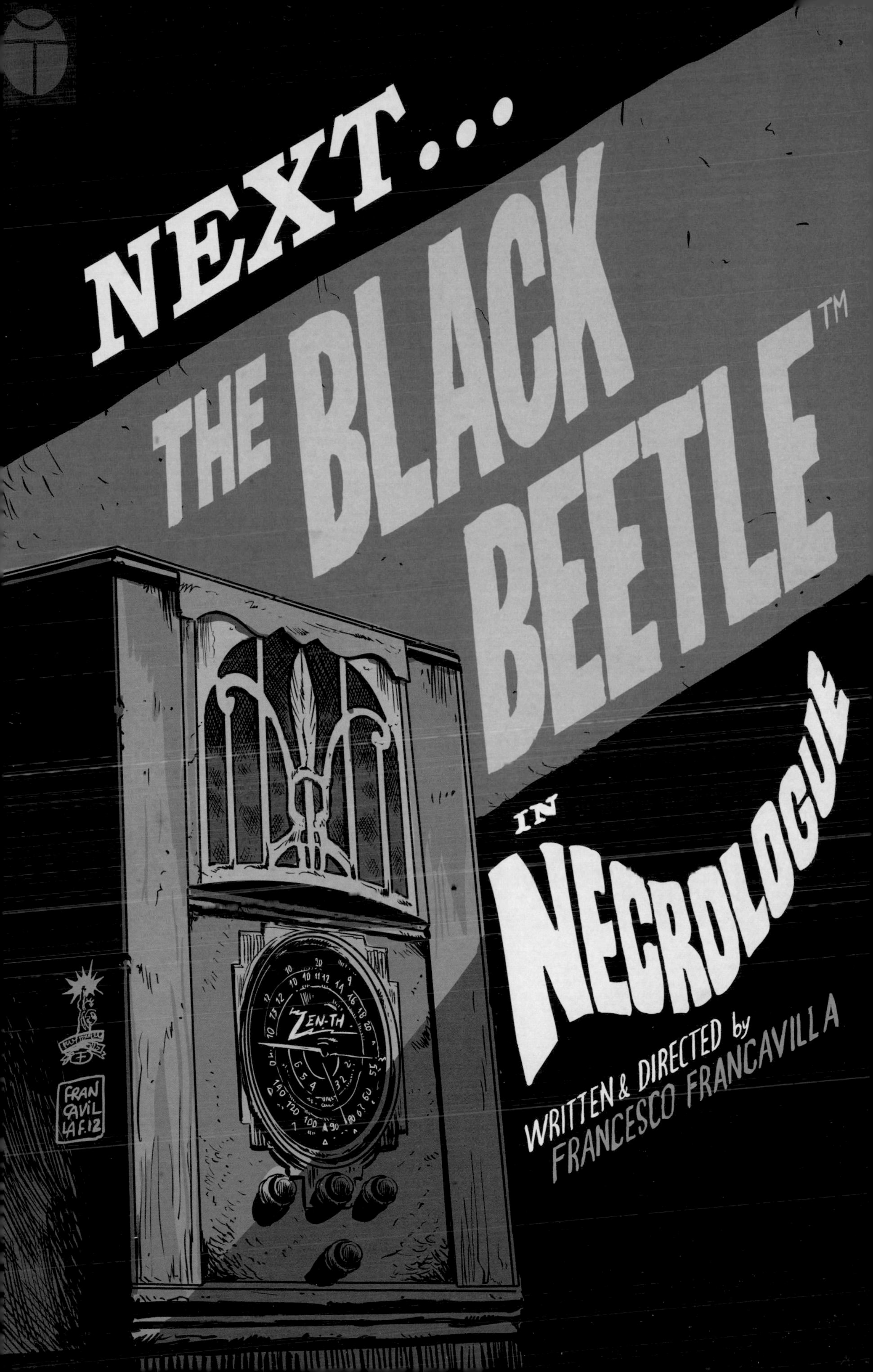
NEXT...
THE BLACK BEETLE™
IN
NECROLOGUE
WRITTEN & DIRECTED by
FRANCESCO FRANCAVILLA
ZEN-TH
FRAN CAVIL LA F.12

RECOMMENDED READING

**THE BLACK BEETLE
VOLUME 1: NO WAY OUT**
Story and art by Francesco Francavilla
978-1-61655-202-2 | $19.99

THE GUILD LIBRARY EDITION
Story by Felicia Day and others,
art by Francesco Francavilla and others
978-1-61655-983-0 | $49.99

**THE SHAOLIN COWBOY:
SHEMP BUFFET**
Story and art by Geof Darrow
978-1-61655-726-3 | $19.99

**THE UMBRELLA ACADEMY
VOLUME 1: APOCALYPSE SUITE**
Story by Gerard Way, art by Gabriel Bá
978-1-59307-978-9 | $17.99

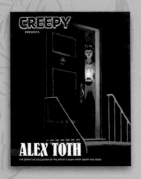

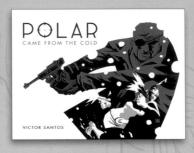

CREEPY PRESENTS ALEX TOTH
Story and art by Alex Toth and others
978-1-61655-692-1 | $19.99

FIGHT CLUB 2 LIBRARY EDITION
Story by Chuck Palahniuk, art by Cameron Stewart
978-1-50670-237-7 | $149.99

**POLAR VOLUME 1:
CAME FROM THE COLD**
Story and art by Victor Santos
978-1-61655-232-9 | $17.99

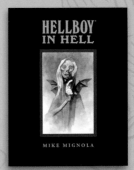

**BLACK HAMMER
VOLUME 1: SECRET ORIGINS**
Story by Jeff Lemire,
art by Dean Ormston
978-1-61655-786-7 | $14.99

ARCHIE VS. PREDATOR
Story by Alex de Campi,
art by Fernando Ruiz
and Rich Koslowski
978-1-61655-805-5 | $19.99

**LOBSTER JOHNSON
VOLUME 2: THE BURNING HAND**
Story by Mike Mignola and John Arcudi,
art by Tonci Zonjic
978-1-61655-031-8 | $17.99

**HELLBOY IN HELL
LIBRARY EDITION**
Story and art by Mike Mignola
978-1-50670-363-3 | $49.99

The Black Beetle™ © Francesco Francavilla. The Guild™ © The Knights of Good Productions. The Shaolin Cowboy™ © Geof Darrow. Creepy ™ & © New Comic Company. Polar™ © Victor Santos. Fight Club 2™ © Chuck Palahniuk. The Umbrella Academy™ © Gerard Way and Gabriel Bá. Mike Mignola's Hellboy™ and Lobster Johnson™ © Michael Mignola. Black Hammer™ © 171 Studios, Inc., and Dean Ormston. Archie™ and © Archie Comic Publications, Inc. Predator™ and © Twentieth Century Fox Film Corporation. Dark Horse Books® and the Dark Horse logo are registered trademarks of Dark Horse Comics, Inc. All rights reserved.

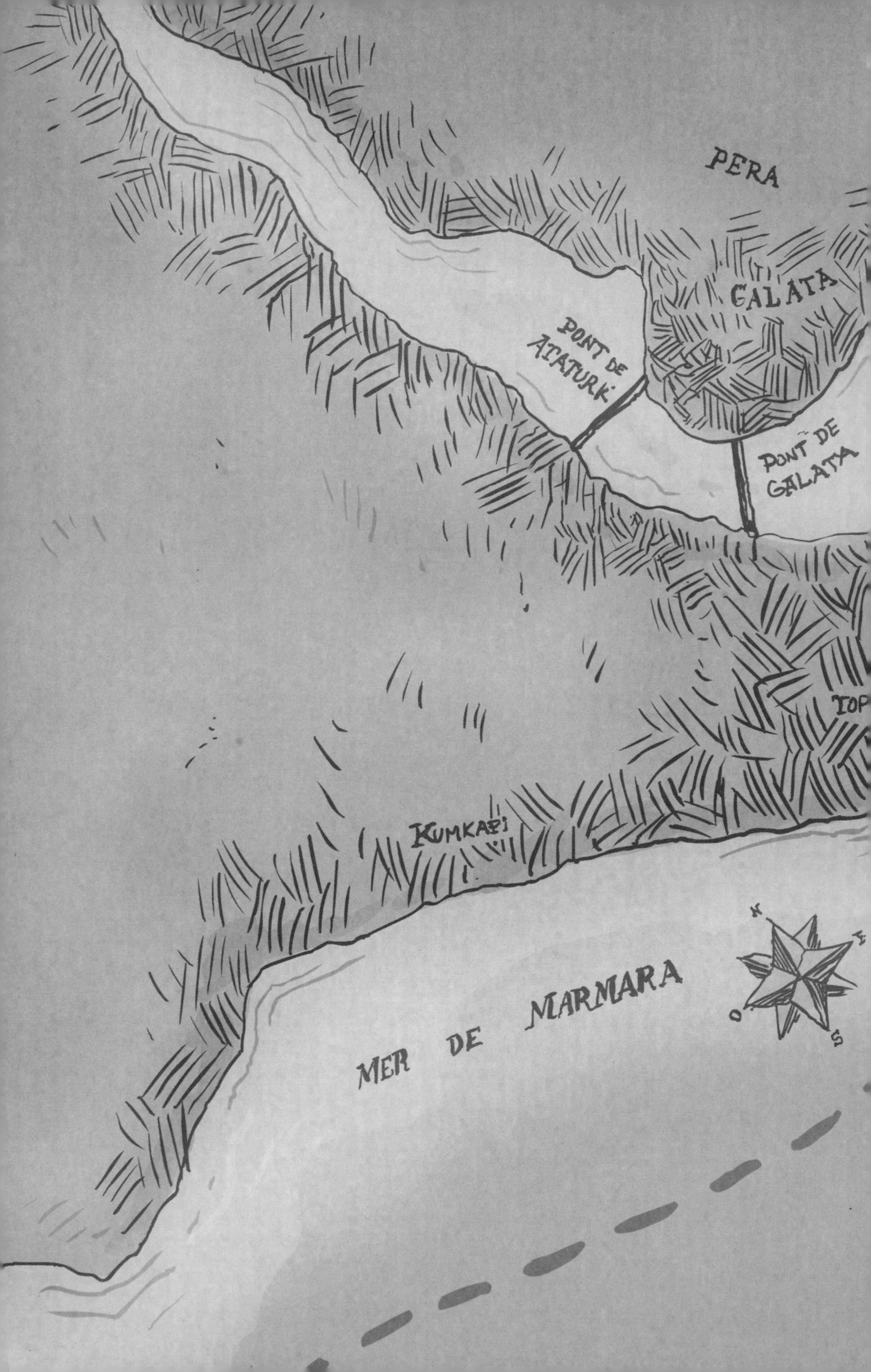
PERA
GALATA
PONT DE ATATURK
PONT DE GALATA
TOP
KUMKAPI
MER DE MARMARA
N
E
S
O